John and William Bartram
Travelers in Early America

John and William Bartram
Travelers in Early America

Enjoy!
Sandra Wallus Sammons
March '08

Sandra Wallus Sammons

Ocean Publishing
Flagler Beach, Florida

John and William Bartram
Travelers in Early America

By Sandra Wallus Sammons

Published by:
Ocean Publishing
Post Office Box 1080
Flagler Beach, Florida 32136 U.S.A.
orders@ocean-publishing.com
www.ocean-publishing.com

ISBN, print ed.   0-9717641-2-3
LCCN   2004100054

Printed and bound in the United States of America.

Dedication

For Aja Marie Sammons,

        as she approaches her
        own new world...

"This world, as a glorious apartment of the boundless palace of the sovereign Creator, is furnished with an infinite variety of animated scenes, inexpressibly beautiful and pleasing, equally free to the inspection and enjoyment of all his creatures."

William Bartram
Travels

Acknowledgements

Thanks to all at Historic Bartram's Garden in Philadelphia, especially Joel T. Fry, Curator of Historic Collections.

Thanks for comments made by Edward J. Cashin, Director of the Center for the Study of Georgia History, and author of *William Bartram and the American Revolution on the Southern Frontier;* and Brad Sanders, teacher, and author of *Guide to William Bartram's Travels*.

All the librarians at Edgewater Public Library were invaluable, with special thanks to Anne Potter for the constant flow of inter-library loan books.

Bob Sammons, Elsie Wallus and Joan Teta all made excellent suggestions. Author Elizabeth Vollstadt, Dee Hamma, Sharon Brammer, and Donna Martin lent their support to the project.

Librarian Dana Thompson and teachers Connie McKenzie, Joe Vetter, and Christopher Weinrich considered suitability in the schools. Students Aja Sammons, Katharine Walker, T. J. Masters, and Brooke Elmore gave other excellent comments.

Special thanks to Frank Gromling, my publisher, for understanding that this book was needed.

Appreciation goes to the following publishers for allowing us to use brief excerpts from these published works:

Billy Bartram and His Green World, Dorothy Sanger, 1972, Farrar, Straus & Giroux.

The Correspondence of John Bartram, 1734-1777, Berkeley, Edmund and Dorothy Berkeley, 1992, University Press of Florida.

The Life and Letters of Alexander Wilson, Clark Hunter, 1983, Memoirs of the American Philosophical Society, Vol. 154.

The Life and Travels of John Bartram: From Lake Ontario to the River Saint John, Edmund Berkeley, 1990, University Press of Florida.

The Natures of John and William Bartram, Thomas P. Slaughter, 1996, Random House.

William Bartram and the American Revolution on the Southern Frontier, Edward J. Cashin, 2000, University of South Carolina Press.

Travels, William Bartram, 1966, The Library of America.

Walden, Henry David Thoreau, 1997, Beacon Press.

Appreciation also goes to the following organizations for photographic permissions:

South Carolina Historical Society, Charleston, SC.

Historic Bartram's Garden, Philadelphia, PA.

Independence National Historical Park – Library, Philadelphia, PA.

The Historical Society of Pennsylvania, Philadelphia, PA.

The Natural History Museum, London, England

John and William Bartram: Travelers in Early America

Notes to Readers

Quotes in the book are reproduced from the writing of the time. Therefore, either from the original author's haste, or from different rules of grammar at the time, the spelling and punctuation may not be the same as ours today.

Also, in colonial days, the city of Charleston, South Carolina, was called Charles Town, but the current name has been used for clarity in the text.

The Bartram House
Philadelphia, Pennsylvania
Courtesy: Sandra Wallus Sammons

John and William Bartram: Travelers in Early America

Table of Contents

Foreword by Joel T. Fry, Curator of Historic Collections,
Historic Bartram's Garden

Foreword

The work of John and William Bartram – America's first native botanists, father and son travelers, plant hunters, and master gardeners – should be well known. The story of their lives is full of adventure and unbridled curiosity, but too often it has fallen through the cracks of history. Their love of nature and science has been lost to a world that sees history as a tabulation of political or military events.

There has been a gradual re-discovery of John and William Bartram over the last few years. Beginning with Francis Harper's work to trace their routes through Florida and the South, it is now possible to visit places they described and experience the nature they loved. But following the Bartram trails also emphasize the changes that have happened over two centuries. Much of the wild world the Bartrams explored is now gone.

Sandy Sammons' book fills a real need – a book to interest young readers in the lives of John and William Bartram. The Bartram story is complex, but Sammons has managed to tell the story in a compelling fashion. She has captured the spirit of John and William Bartram with great skill. We can hope it will spread a love of John and William Bartram's world beyond the 21st century.

Joel T. Fry, Curator
Historic Bartram's Garden
Philadelphia, Pennsylvania

Preface

I was in an airplane flying at more than 30,000 feet above the earth, returning home from a research trip to Historic Bartram's Garden in Philadelphia, Pennsylvania. Heading south to Florida, the clouds parted for a very clear view of the Great Smoky Mountains of Tennessee and Blue Ridge Mountains of North Carolina. The mountains gave way to rolling hills in Georgia, and I could easily see the meanderings of small rivers like the Altamaha and its tributaries. As the woman next to me was working on her laptop computer, I was suddenly struck by the huge difference 300 years had made.

It took me just a few hours to go over one thousand miles in the twenty-first century; in the eighteenth century travel was by foot or horseback or boat, so fifty miles was a good day's journey. To tell my publisher about my trip, e-mail and telephone were handy when I arrived home; John Bartram would have hand-written a letter, keeping a copy for himself for when he received a reply — two months later.

John Bartram lived and traveled along the East Coast of colonial America during the 1700s. The early settlers shared the land with Native Americans who had lived here for thousands of years before the arrival of the Europeans. There were footpaths or rivers through the thick woods connecting one small village to the next. The land overflowed with wildlife: life-threatening or peace-loving animals, huge flocks of noisy birds, and fish so plentiful that they filled the rivers. Trees and shrubs of all sizes and shapes and scents filled the forests. Anyone interested in exploring that forbidding but fascinating wilderness would have been endlessly fascinated.

John Bartram caught that fascination and became one of America's earliest botanists. Going beyond the study of plants, his intense curiosity led him to question everything around him, allowing the whole natural world to be his own open-air school. John transplanted wild plants into his botanic garden (one of the first in America) and then sold many of them to Europe, starting a trans-Atlantic correspondence that would add tremendously to the scientific thinking of his time. John's reputation grew with his garden's size and variety.

John's son, William, absorbed his father's love of nature, but found his own very individual path through life. Sidetracked for years, this artist was determined to express his own inner talent. He is now remembered not only for his art, but also for his work with plants and birds, and for one very special book. William influenced many other artists and writers because he clung fast to his own inner dream.

Both men were pioneers. In their own very distinct ways, they entered unknown territories and blazed trails for those who came after them. Travel with me now, back to the time when America was full of plants, just waiting to be discovered...

Chapter 1
Beginnings in a New Land

"Land! Land!" The sailors and passengers aboard the *Welcome* were filled with excitement. After their long, exhausting voyage from England, they finally spotted the land called America. It was October, and thousands of trees were ablaze with color. The *Welcome* was bringing new settlers to Pennsylvania, one of Great Britain's new colonies across the Atlantic Ocean. William Penn, for whom Pennsylvania ("Penn's Woods") had been named, was among those on board.

This 1682 crossing would be the first of many, for the colony was to be a "holy experiment."[1] Many on these ships were Quakers, members of a religious group that had grown in large numbers in England. They had been persecuted because their faith was different from the Church of England.

William Penn, also a Quaker, had promised that everyone in his colony, even Native Americans already living in the area, would be treated fairly.

> **Quakers** – The Religious Society of Friends, or Quakers, believe that one way to show respect for God is to protect and preserve nature, which is God's creation. Believers are expected to treat every human being as a child of God, overcome evil with good, and not resort to physical violence.

When John Bartram's grandfather and grandmother came to the Pennsylvania colony a year later, they found excellent farmland in Darby, just a few miles from the very small town of Philadelphia. Deciding to settle there, they built a house and barn, and greeted their few neighbors. A short distance away, the Lenni-Lenape Indians (also called the Delawares) lived in their own villages.

Expanded view showing the Bartram land

A plan of the City of Philadelphia (1777), showing the Bartram land
Courtesy: The John Bartram Association, Historic Bartram's Garden

When John Bartram's father and mother married, they too lived in Darby. On a fresh spring day, May 23, 1699, John Bartram was born. The cold of winter was fading and buds were opening into green leaves on the trees. The new Pennsylvania colony and the Bartram family were both full of possibilities for the future.

In those early days of the colonies, however, there was also reason for fear. Women gave birth at home, and when John was only two years old, his mother died a short time after the birth of his brother James. John's father later remarried, had two more children, and moved to North Carolina. When John was ten years old his father also died, killed in an Indian raid.

John Bartram lived on his grandparents' farm and attended the Darby Meeting School, where he received a good basic education. For eight hours each day, five days a week, then four more hours on Saturdays, students learned reading, writing, and arithmetic, and about the Quaker religion. When students reached the age of twelve, schooling usually stopped, because children of that age were needed on the farm. John became a farmer, as did most of the young men at that time.

On April 25, 1723, at age 23, John Bartram married Mary Maris and they started their own family. They had two sons and made plans for a happy future in Darby. Again tragedy struck. Mary died in 1727, possibly from complications at childbirth, and their first son Richard also died soon afterward. John was left alone to care for their second child, Isaac.

The farmer immersed himself in his work, but questions kept popping into his mind. He had always been interested in plants, but now he wanted to learn more. John knew that some plants were used as medicines. Was it possible that any of these plants might have cured his Mary or Richard? Why does one plant grow faster than another, even though they're in the same field? There were few books in the colonies, and not many at all on plants. Most of the other settlers weren't interested in the names of the trees or plants growing around them. They cut down trees and plowed up plants so they could build houses and grow gardens.

In trying to find answers to his many questions, John the farmer was growing, as well. He was evolving from a farmer into a botanist. A farmer puts seeds into the ground and helps them grow; a botanist studies the seeds and plants to understand why and how they grow.

A story was told about John's tremendous interest in all of nature. While plowing a field, he looked down at a daisy growing among the rocks and clods of dirt. He picked up the flower and realized that although he had noticed plants like this before, he really had not seen the detail of it. This common little daisy was fascinating! One small plant, thought of as a weed, had a very obvious order in each of its petals and leaves. There is true beauty in nature! There is order in nature! John Bartram resolved to learn everything he possibly could about the nature all around him.

John had inherited the 200-acre family farm at Darby, but in 1728 found land in Kingsessing, nearer to the growing city of Philadelphia, that he would live on for the rest of his life. He bought over 100 acres of rolling meadow and woods, with a small house, along the west bank of the clear, clean, Schuylkill River. Schuylkill means "hidden river" in Dutch, and his new home had a delightful setting. The Schuylkill was a busy river, with boats being a major means of transportation in the early eighteenth century.

John Bartram found happiness in Kingsessing. In December 1729, he married Ann Mendenhall and soon built a new stone house, which was expanded and modified over the years. Isaac would have plenty of brothers and sisters: James, Moses, Elizabeth (who died when she was a baby), Mary, twins William and another Elizabeth, Ann, John (later called Johnny), and Benjamin. Showing his happiness for all the world to see, John carved "John Ann Bartram 1731" in one of the stones of the house, above an attic window.

Ann Bartram stayed busy. In addition to raising nine lively children, she took care of the vegetables and herbs in the kitchen garden, milked the cows, and fed the poultry. When John built a springhouse (a small shed built over a stream to keep foods cold), Ann kept milk, butter, and cheese there to keep it cool for her family. During the winter she did her spinning of wool and sewing of clothing. Ann shared her husband's interest in the natural world around her, and their sons and daughters followed in their footsteps. She helped John with his chosen work and the couple had a happy marriage.

John worked steadily at his farming, but his growing curiosity would soon make him the talk of the town. He tried various fertilizers and probably rotated his crops, planting different seeds each year in the same field, thereby enriching the soil. He may have been the first in Pennsylvania to do soil testing to see where plants would grow best. He was one of the first conservationists, believing that trees cut down should be replaced elsewhere. Along with his neighbors, he drained marshland near the river so that more of his acreage would be useful. He created a pond in which he could keep turtles, frogs, fish and water plants. People soon came from miles around to see why John Bartram was harvesting larger crops than the farmers around him.

Curiosity pushed him even further. Noticing some interesting plants outside of his garden, he dug them up and transplanted them into several acres he set aside as a special botanic garden, later calling it his "garden of delight."[2] The ever-questioning botanist then studied each new specimen and tried to grow new plants from their seeds. In search of ever more wild plants, he explored the deeper woods around the farm. He was hooked, and when Ann rang the dinner bell some evenings, she never knew from what direction John would come!

There was much danger in the woods. All the animals – including bears, wolves, rattlesnakes, –

had lived undisturbed for many years. Staying very alert, John rode into the woods on his horse, often alone, ever in search of a new plant he could add to his botanic garden. When an interesting specimen caught his attention, he tied a bell around his horse's neck, let the horse roam free, and wandered to his heart's content. When deepening shadows indicated the day was almost over, they finally headed home, with the horse loaded down with overstuffed saddlebags. In the beginning, John collected to satisfy his own curiosity, but as others also became interested in these unusual plants, he started selling some to neighbors and to small commercial nurseries that were starting up in America.

His horizons were ever-expanding, and each fascinating new specimen led to more questions. Some plants flowered; some did not. Some had large leaves; some were tiny. The more variety he saw in nature, the more he wanted to understand the similarities and differences of the plants in his precious garden. His friends were glad to help.

John found that many other people in the fast-developing city of Philadelphia were also interested in botany and natural science. Joseph Breintnall, a Quaker merchant who from 1735 to 1738 was also sheriff of Philadelphia, had a fascinating hobby. At that time, there was no easy way to make a copy of an object, so he made impressions of leaves on paper, showing great detail. Breintnall gratefully accepted leaves from John's new discoveries when the botanist came into town, but Breintnall also visited John in his garden, where they spent many hours sharing ideas about nature and the world around them.

> **Breintnall** – Joseph Breintnall practiced an ancient art of reproducing the detail of a leaf by coating it with printer's ink and pressing it onto a piece of absorbent paper.

One day Breintnall was visited by Dr. Samuel Chew, a physician who recently had moved to Philadelphia. Because doctors at that time relied on plants for medications, Dr. Chew was very interested in the variety of Breintnall's collection of leaves. When their conversation turned to the source of his large collection, Breintnall gladly told Dr. Chew about his amazing friend John Bartram. Excited by this news, Dr. Chew returned home and immediately wrote a letter to an acquaintance in London, England, about this American with a zest for finding new plants.

Dr. Chew's friend was Peter Collinson, another Quaker, whose interest in botany had started at a young age. For his career, he became a merchant in his father's business in London, selling quality fabrics in England and the colonies. For his own pleasure, however, he also had a country house with an exquisite garden. Gardens were very popular in England at that time, and Collinson's dream was to have the best.

Peter Collinson, 1770
Courtesy: The John Bartram Association, Historic Bartram's Garden

Several times Collinson had expressed an interest to Dr. Chew and others that he wanted plants from America. He desired an exchange, so that when American plants were received, interesting English specimens would be sent in return. Collinson realized, too, being a businessman, that many other Englishmen were also interested in plants that grew in America. He had been frustrated in his efforts to find a reliable American collector, though – until he heard about John Bartram.

John and William Bartram: Travelers in Early America

Chapter 2
Growing Gardens and Friendships

John Bartram and Peter Collinson started writing letters to each other in the early 1730s, and although they would never meet in person, their shared enthusiasm and love of nature would change the world around them. For over thirty years, their relationship grew from two men who shared a hobby, to very close friends who were partners in a business that was exciting and profitable to both. Letters and packages exchanged between Bartram, in a small British colony in America, and Collinson, in a large city in Great Britain, would add greatly to the whole scientific learning of their time.

With the encouragement of his new friend, John Bartram started traveling farther away from his farm. Scheduling his adventures around his farm chores, he left the Philadelphia area for the first time in the mid-1730s. He went across the Delaware River into the swamps of New Jersey, looking for evergreen trees he had heard were there. He found long-coned white pine and white cedar trees, among other new plants. When packages were sent to London, Collinson was constantly amazed at the fascinating variety in each delivery.

Collinson was very aware of the dangers his friend faced on longer trips. He honestly admitted that he could never do such risky work. When John mentioned plans for a trip that same year along the Schuylkill River in Pennsylvania, tracing it to its source, advice was quickly sent: three horses should be taken on the trip, one for himself, one for his servant, and one on which to carry the many new specimens. John read the letter, but he knew exactly what to take – one horse, sturdy shoes, and large saddlebags.

More advice was given when John mentioned a trip to the southern colonies. Collinson, just five years older than John, felt free to write: "...pray go very Clean, neat & handsomely Dressed to Virginia...."[1] John, treasuring their friendship, took the comments good-naturedly.

Collinson's very good friend Lord Petre was also interested in buying some American plants for his own garden. Together, they sent John a compass and sundial, which allowed John to be clearer as to direction and correct time of day during his travels. Because John wrote the details in journals along his way and sent the information to Collinson in his letters, the more accurate reporting was beneficial to all. John's trip of almost three hundred miles along the Schuylkill River was successful, and both saddlebags and journal were full on his return home.

John sent seeds and small plants to Collinson, and in exchange, his English friend sent a calico gown for Ann, cloth for a suit for John, gifts for the children, and interesting English plants. There was satisfaction on both sides of the Atlantic, with Collinson so excited about the packages that he opened each one himself. He wouldn't trust his servants to touch his treasures, not after his American friend had taken such pains to collect and send them. The Englishman got down in the dirt and even did the planting himself, thoroughly enjoying being outside for a while with birds chirping around him. Although each package came with a detailed list of its contents, Collinson learned to be very careful with every bit of soil around each plant. There were times when he found a bonus, such as a tiny wildflower or moss that had attached itself to a root.

Sharing of plants blossomed into a time-consuming job, however, as Collinson shared with more friends about his source for the new trees and shrubs in his garden. He found himself increasingly pressed for time, trying to find time for both business and botany. There were times when he would stand at his busy counter, quill pen in hand, writing a quick note to send to America or friends all over Europe who had been informed of the bounty coming from Pennsylvania. John Bartram had the same problem. He had to fit letter writing in between trips, farm work, and the needs of his family. Both correspondents would often write on Sundays or at night, by candlelight. Once when Collinson was writing at night, he remarked: "Don't it make thee smile – I sett out to say little & now I scrawl on for I know how thou loves long stories – It's past 10:00 so good night ...."[2]

The communication on both sides was enjoyed tremendously although the flow was not always smooth. Sometimes several letters would be answered in one long response. In October of 1759 Collinson wrote to John: "I received my Dear John's letter of the 16th June. His hodge podge digests very well with me. I may give him as good as he sends ...."[3]

It was important, therefore, to keep a copy of each letter, so John would usually keep his quick draft, then write a cleaner, neater copy to send. The pleasant but time-consuming chore of writing letters increased tremendously over the years as John was introduced by Collinson to some of the most brilliant people in America and Europe.

Sir Hans Sloane, a London physician, author, and collector of a great variety of natural specimens, corresponded with John Bartram, the self-taught American botanist. Philip Miller, the Gardener for the Physic Garden of medicinal plants at Chelsea in London, and author of the *Gardener's Dictionary*, was grateful to receive some of John's plants. Dutch physician and naturalist John Gronovius was already familiar with some American species. He had edited and published John Clayton's book on plants of the Virginia colony. German-born John Dillenius, of Oxford, taught the American botanist about lichens and mosses in exchange for interesting specimens.

Carl Linnaeus, the Swedish botanist, had created a modern system of classifying plants, but was always interested in seeing new varieties. Even though he never traveled outside his own country, John Bartram's reputation spread far and wide.

Naming of Plants – To botanists of the 1700s and 1800s, naming plants was very important. Some people were honored by having plants named for them: the gardenia for Dr. Alexander Garden; the mountain laurel was named the *kalmia latifolia* for Peter Kalm; the *collinsonia* for Peter Collinson; and William named the *fothergilla* for Dr. John Fothergill. A moss called *bartramia* and the Bartram oak were named for the Bartrams.

Great care was given to the packaging of bulbs, seeds, roots and plants to be sent overseas. Even placing the specimens in his sturdy homemade boxes and in the driest moss would not always ensure a safe delivery. Rats loved digging into the boxes to start nests. Salt water might drench a package, turning the plants brown and withered. Ships were often delayed in port, and seeds would sprout and rot. Both sides tried to find the best way to protect their precious cargo. Plants with their roots tucked into an ox bladder would stay fresh, and fresh fruit or vegetables should *never* be sent right in with the plants!

Even letters were not exempt from the trials and tribulations of shipping. Collinson wrote: "I have much to do to read thy Letter for some Mischievous Insect has Eaten thy Letter in large holes..."[4] Before an organized mail delivery system was in place, even mail within the colonies had its own peculiar problems.

Depending on a friend to deliver something in another colony might work, but the item might also be forgotten for months.

Successes more than made up for failures, however. When a package did arrive safely across the ocean, there could be quite a surprise inside. John sent a box of turtle eggs to England. His timing was excellent. When the package was opened, baby turtles were just scrambling out of their shells. "... [T]hey have had many Visitors,"⁵ Collinson wrote back to John, excitedly showing off his brand new American baby turtles to anyone who came along. Another time John sent a live Mud Turtle, but Collinson didn't want another, thank you.

Patience was also a virtue in their exchanges. Some of the specimens John sent across the ocean took time to mature in another climate. Collinson was ecstatic when, after about twenty years of pampering a mountain magnolia, the tree finally had flowers. "... I presume [it] is the first of that species that ever flowered in England..."⁶ he proudly wrote to John.

Collinson loved the plants, but through the years he made it very clear that they were not his only interest. John, also interested in everything around him, agreed. "Every uncommon thing thou finds in any branch of Nature, will be acceptable,"⁷ Collinson wrote. When John complied and continually sent a huge variety of specimens and information, Collinson gratefully said: "... upon my Word Friend John I can't help Admiring thy Abilities in so many Instances."⁸

One letter from John was about the mouth of a rattlesnake. John had come upon a dead rattler in the woods, and took the time to do a very careful and detailed study of how the fangs and hinged jaws worked. He was fascinated, and knew his English friend would be, too. Peter Collinson was a member of the Royal Society of London, an organization of men who enjoyed scientific studies, and he shared John's letter with the other members at one of their meetings. Delighted with the new information, the letter was also accepted for publication in their yearly publication, the *Transactions* of the Royal Society. John's discoveries about wasps, dragonflies, caterpillars, and the seventeen-year locust were also printed in other issues of the *Transactions* through the years. John Bartram's fame continued to spread.

The eighteenth century was a time of reason and enlightenment. Like a fresh breeze after the unquestioning thinking of the past, scientists started to look closely at the world around them and come up with logical answers. By 1700, it had only been about twenty years since men had proved that insects came, not from mud, but from eggs. Sir Isaac Newton was just about to explain that objects fall to the ground because of gravity. Thinking men would no longer just accept their surroundings. The time had come to observe, evaluate, measure, experiment, and label what they saw with opened eyes.

Curious men asked how a rattlesnake kills its prey. They wanted to know for sure if the snake charms its prey first and then strikes, or if it bites first, releasing poison into its victim. They wanted to know where birds go in winter. Some said they go to a warmer climate, and some said they go underwater. They wanted to know if there were really such creatures as unicorns and dragons. Realizing that no one person could have all the answers, interested men (and a few women) around the world freely, openly, and enthusiastically shared their thoughts, not stopping until they had logical, provable answers.

To spread new ideas in America, John Bartram and Benjamin Franklin discussed starting a group in the colonies like the Royal Society in London and the Boston Medical Society in the Massachusetts colony. Franklin, with John's suggestions, wrote up the guidelines. The small group, called the American Philosophical Society, met in 1744 in Philadelphia. John Bartram represented botanical studies, while others would discuss geography, chemistry, and other subjects. A president and treasurer were chosen, and Benjamin Franklin was secretary. It was another first for the blossoming colonies.

This openness led to very practical help for scientists everywhere. Experiments with electricity were still primitive when Benjamin Franklin became fascinated with the subject. After writing to Collinson about his experiments, he was sent some equipment as well as the latest information from scientists in Europe on the subject. Collinson also forwarded Franklin's new discoveries to the Royal Society, where Franklin received even more encouragement to proceed.

Benjamin Franklin, just six years younger than his good friend John Bartram, was a printer by trade and very active in Philadelphia. He started a group called the Junto, which organized an academy, hospital, subscription library, and fire department in Philadelphia, all of which helped make the city a center for learning and culture. Collinson helped by sending books for the new library, and John Bartram, because of his high regard in the scientific community, was allowed free use of the book collection.

> **Junto** – Junto comes from a Spanish word meaning committee, or council. Franklin's Junto, started in 1727, was a place where men could debate questions about botany, philosophy, and other subjects. They debated only to pursue truth, not to win a contest.

John Bartram loved books. Collinson and other scientists sent some books directly to the botanist, at times as payment for his plants. John kept his precious books, such as Henry Baker's *The Microscope Made Easy*, in "… my little library or Chapel as I call it …."[9] He would sometimes even read while eating, with spoon in one hand and book in the other, ceaseless in his quest for knowledge.

Another place where John might find much information was at James Logan's home in Philadelphia. Logan, who was an avid reader, served as secretary to William Penn and later became acting governor of the colony. He had amassed the largest collection of books in the city, with more than 2,000 books in his private library. Glad to loan books to John Bartram, he also took the time to explain some of the technical language. He helped John with his Latin, and when he received a copy of the new plant classification system published by Carl Linnaeus, also explained that to John. When Collinson sent John a microscope, Logan demonstrated its use. Impressed with his desire to learn, Logan once said that John Bartram "...had a genius perfectly well turned for botany."[10]

Chapter 3
"All in a flame"

With all his busyness, however, John did not neglect his family or farm. He took an active interest in each of the children as they matured, even taking several of them on short plant-finding trips. As the farm prospered, he bought more land and hired help during seed times and harvest. Because Quaker beliefs teach the equality of all people, everyone would eat at the same table at the Bartram home. John, Ann, their children, and Harvey, their freed slave, would be together at mealtimes. John still planned his trips for plants around his farm chores, and Harvey managed the farm while John was away.

When his restless spirit could roam, however, one trip led to another. In 1737 and 1738, John traveled to Delaware, Maryland and Virginia, explored the Chesapeake Bay, and climbed into caves in the Blue Ridge Mountains just to see what was inside. The vivid autumn color on the mountains and the cool crisp fall air were invigorating. He covered more than 1,000 miles but the trips went by quickly. After climbing mountains and combing seashores, John returned home ready to rest – and then, to go again.

Each exploratory journey only raised his, and Collinson's, curiosity level, prodding him on to another, even longer adventure. By 1739 he had again gone beyond just identifying and collecting plants. He wrote of "... severall successful experiments of joining several species of ye same genus whereby I have obtained curious mixed colours in flowers never known before ...."[1] He was an experimental botanist, crossbreeding different plants, and became one of the first people in America to experiment with hybridizing plants.

Out on a collecting trip, John would sometimes have a guide, but it was often easier to travel alone. Collinson, always trying to help, would try to send letters ahead of time, informing him of friends or business acquaintances along his route. John then not only had places to stay, but he met people who understood and appreciated the purpose of his trip.

John said: "I am now all in A flame ...."[2] to go on a trip, but his chosen life was not easy. Weather and Indians were a problem. One fall he went out to gather seeds of an evergreen and stood in snow up to his knees picking off pine cones. Knowing that his father had died at the hands of unfriendly Indians also caused John much worry. He came to the conclusion that the only way to deal with Indians was to "... bang them stoutly. "[3]

Mountain climbing was another challenge. Planning a trip to New York in 1741, John was after the seeds of balsam fir trees that he knew he would find near the tops of the Catskill Mountains. Collinson and others in Europe wanted these trees because of their wonderful scent. John had a rough time climbing up and over the sharp rocks and slippery slopes. Late one afternoon, while bagging his prized seeds, he suddenly realized that darkness was fast approaching. Deciding not to spend the night on the mountain, he rushed to reach safety in the valley below. As he ran through the thick woods, "... it was so dark before I reached ye bottom that I could hardly see ye brambles or rocks before I run against them."[4]

Usually John's routines worked out quite well. He still brought only one horse with him, outfitted with two saddlebags. He took a roll of bedding, a change of clothes, some tools, a gun for hunting, and perhaps a reference book or two. A few items were necessary for cooking, such as salt and flour, but for the most part he ate what he found on the trail. Nuts, fruits, berries, small game, and fish were delicious and gave him energy for the trip.

Invited on a six-week trip to a meeting with the tribes of the Iroquois Nation in western New York in 1743, John traveled safely with other members of their group in the presence of Conrad Weiser, agent and interpreter for the Indians. A meeting with the Indians was held in Onondaga, the capital of the Iroquois Nation, close to Lake Ontario and the Canadian border. New boundary lines were being drawn, again leaving the Native Americans less for their own hunting grounds. Later John would say about the Indians of that time: "… thay watch all our motions even our eyes if we look at A Compass thay think we are searching thair Land to Posses it."[5] While talks went on about new boundaries, John spent every spare minute collecting plants and exploring an area that few had seen before.

Some of John's trips deeply impressed his neighbors and friends. He traveled around the colonies, from north to south, eventually going as far west as the Ohio River, but the idea that he would go into Indian country made him quite a legend in his own time. There he was actually passing the frontier of the English settlements, going into what was a foreign land. Even his good friend, Joseph Breintnall, wrote a poem about John's bravery!

After each of these adventures, package after package was sent to people who were willing to pay for American plants. Both John Bartram and Peter Collinson befriended some of the ship captains who regularly made trips across the Atlantic, asking them to take special care with their shipments. Some captains took the packages into their own cabins, not knowing that there were wasps' nests, sprouting skunk cabbages, snails, or dried birds packed in tobacco dust in the boxes.

During the winter of 1744/1745, John was kicked in the back by his horse. He was so badly bruised that he couldn't even turn over in his bed and had to lie still. He wrote to his friend Collinson: "… I was forced to lie upon my back which was a great affliction to mee who cant rest long without action and who cannot endure confinement...."[6] He was soon up and about again.

Peter Collinson, Benjamin Franklin and others wanted to see John paid enough for his collecting to allow him to spend more time on trips and not have to worry about the farm. Although he didn't get paid on a regular subscription basis for long, John *was* able to get a system to his business. Instead of sending out all the seed of any species, he made sure some were planted in his garden so that plants and seeds would be readily available when requested.

Specific orders required special handling, but for those who simply wanted a representative selection, he could easily put together 100 trees and shrubs in one package, for which he charged one set amount. Life became easier, and the pay he received was enough to allow him to continue searching for that always-elusive brand-new specimen. The constant prodding from his patrons for something new did get tiresome at times, though. He asked Collinson in one letter if his patrons thought he could *make* new plants.

One thing John could always do is ask questions. Always seeking to expand this network of correspondents, John once said: "... I am ready to learn of any learned person that will be so kind as to instruct me in any branch of Natural History which is my beloved amusement."[7] Benjamin Franklin, John's good friend, helped out here. When he became Postmaster in Philadelphia, he let his scientific friends send letters postage-free.

Other "learned persons" were constantly introduced to John by his increasingly large network of friends in Europe and America. He heard about a London physician who was fascinated with geology, the study of rocks and how the earth is formed. John sent Dr. John Fothergill, also a Quaker, some rocks and plants. So began another friendship, one that would be of great help to John not only scientifically, but also for his family in the future.

Mark Catesby, the English-born author of the first major study of plants in the American colonies, *The Natural History of Carolina, Florida and the Bahama Islands*, was always searching for new plant specimens for his books. John corresponded with Catesby on his return to England, with John sending letters and newly-found species, while Catesby sent the latest volumes of his *Natural History*. Because Collinson also knew Catesby, Collinson would sometimes ask John for plants he had seen in Catesby's drawings. Catesby's work would influence later artists, including John James Audubon.

Peter Kalm, the Swedish botanist, was fascinated with John. The American botanist could talk not only about plants. He could discuss almost any subject in nature. John was fascinated with the idea that perhaps oceans had once covered much of the earth. He could find no other explanation for the seashells found in parts of inland Virginia, Maryland, New Jersey, and New York. John believed that there are mountains under the oceans, and that perhaps someday someone would discover them, through soundings from ships. He even suggested that those ridges or mountains under the ocean might affect ocean currents.

These were ideas that would have been advanced for a formally educated scholar. John Bartram was just a self-taught farmer, but with a huge amount of curiosity. Peter Kalm wrote to Carl Linnaeus later saying their friend John was "... everything, farmer, joiner, turner, shoe-maker, bricklayer, gardener, minister, carpenter, and I don't know what else, a brilliant fellow."[8]

John was not, however, a weeder. Friends were sometimes surprised at the amount of weeds that grew heartily along with the transplanted or propagated shrubs. Again, John graciously listened, but went on doing what he knew was important.

The weeds could wait. He had a very special son to enjoy.

Chapter 4
William, "my little botanist"

William Bartram was born, with his twin sister Elizabeth, on April 20, 1739. William blended in with his many brothers and sisters while growing up on the Bartram farm, but John and Ann Bartram soon recognized that William had a special talent. William amused himself for long periods of time with just some pencils and scraps of paper. He showed a true love of nature, following right in his father's path, and had the added gift of being an artist.

Because of this talent, William was the only one of the Bartram children sent for extra schooling. In 1752, at age 13, William attended the Philadelphia Academy, which had been started by Benjamin Franklin and the Junto. Because it was designed for students who wanted a career in something other than farming, classes offered at the Academy were: Latin, Greek, German, English, History, Geography, Logic, Writing, Astronomy, Drawing, and other subjects.

Academy – Franklin's Academy was not to teach young men to become ministers, or to increase family prestige. This school was different because it was practical for Americans, and emphasized a love of learning. English was actually taught as a language, along with the traditional Latin and Greek. No degrees were given. The academy later became the College of Philadelphia, which was eventually absorbed into the University of Pennsylvania.

Along with the advantage of attending the Academy with its excellent teachers, William, with his brothers and sisters, learned from the many friends his father invited to their home, and from the books in his father's library. Two artists who particularly captured William's imagination were Mark Catesby and George Edwards, and he would learn a lot from seeing their work.

Because his academic studies did not keep him busy all year, the young artist still had time to do what he liked best – drawing and studying the nature around him. By the time he was fifteen he knew most of the plants around their home and had drawn many of the local trees and birds. His father was so impressed that he sent some sketches to Peter Collinson. The Englishman wrote back, saying that Billy's "... pretty performances please Mee Much."[1]

John realized that his plant-collecting trips would be enhanced by the company of this talented son, whom he called "... my little botanist."[2] When William was fourteen the two took trips together to the Catskill Mountains in the New York colony, sharing one exciting experience after another.

Not every experience was pleasant, however. One night shortly into the trip, they found a hut where they could spend the night. They were glad to have shelter, but it was "... hardly big enough for A hen roost."[3] They slept on the floor and shared the space with five or six other travelers — and thousands of lice. At daybreak, they were up and very relieved to be on their way.

Walking along a path, William saw what he thought was a large mushroom. He was about to kick it when he realized – just barely in time – that it was a rattlesnake. He cautioned his father, and instead of slithering away, the snake stayed in a circle to protect itself. Fearlessly approaching, the two cautiously went closer, but stopped at a safe distance from the snake. With a long branch, John tried to persuade the snake to uncoil by prodding it gently. The snake only coiled more tightly, but in doing so, it swelled up and showed them an even brighter display of its colors. Unfortunately, William had forgotten his drawing materials and couldn't draw the live snake, but he didn't miss many opportunities like that.

John always encouraged his son to draw and paint live animals in their own habitat. Drawing from nature, and not from books, was the way to make his illustrations true to life. William practiced and his subjects soon looked as if they could leap off the page.

> **Drawing** – Paper was expensive, and sometimes hard to get in early America. Artists like Mark Catesby and William Bartram filled one page with lots of information. Male and female birds, a tree associated with that species of bird, the flower and bud and seed of that same tree – all would be drawn on one sheet of paper.

On these trips to New York, John and William met Cadwallader Colden, a physician and later lieutenant governor of New York. John had been anxious to meet this learned man because Collinson had mentioned that this doctor, living in the woods of New York colony, was very interested in nature and science. Colden's daughter, Jane, fifteen years older than William, was also an artist and botanist. They also had the good fortune to meet Dr. Alexander Garden, another physician from Charleston, South Carolina, who was visiting with the Coldens. The Catskill Mountains of New York were fascinating for plant-collecting, but Dr. Garden told John all about the many different flowers and trees in his home colony of South Carolina. John was so intrigued that he made a promise to visit there as soon as possible.

Returning home in late December 1754, however, John and William were alarmed by the news of battles in western Pennsylvania. The French and Indian War had started, with the French and British battling on American soil. In just another twenty years there would be another war in the colonies – a revolution against Great Britain.

John and William, father and son, were growing very close. They took another trip together in 1755 to the northern colonies, this time in the company of one of William's professors at the Academy, Francis Allison. They visited Yale University, which had been founded in 1701, and the whole trip was a great learning experience for William.

John told his friends about how much his son enjoyed his art work, and showed pride in William's talent. William did well at the Academy, but "Botany & drawing are his darling delight,"[4] according to his father.

John was proud. John was also practical. He believed strongly that each of his children should have a career. Now with William almost finished with his studies at the Academy, John wrote to Collinson about his talented son: "My son William is just turned of sixteen it is now time to propose some way for him to get his liveing by... I want to put him to some business by which he may with care & industry get A temperate resonable liveing I am afraid Botany & drawing will not afford him one... pray my dear Peter let me have thy opinion about it....."[5]

There might possibly have been a future for William as an artist in England, but the thinking was different in America. England was a settled country, while America was still a country of pioneers. After all, John had worked long, hard years at farming before he felt free to collect plants for his botanic garden. Hard work, not art work, was rewarded in the colonies.

Collinson suggested that William become a printer. He might be able to use his drawing talents in the printing business, even perhaps learning engraving. William didn't want to do engraving. He wanted to create his own designs and drawings, from nature.

Benjamin Franklin, the publisher of many works, including *Poor Richard's Almanac*, offered to teach William the printing trade. When Franklin said that he was the only printer in the colonies making any money, however, John gave up that idea.

Surveying was another possibility. The colonies were growing and surveyors were needed to come up with exact lines between one town and another. However, when John found out that for every one of those job openings there were at least five applicants for the position, that possibility closed as well.

Dr. Alexander Garden of Charleston had a suggestion. William could live with the Garden family while he studied to become a doctor. John knew William would approve of that idea, but for the wrong reason. He was sure William just wanted to learn more about botany from Dr. Garden!

While John was busy thinking, Collinson kept sending pencils, sketching paper, and paints to the young man, still encouraging him to draw. He showed William's drawings to many people, and the drawings brought nothing but praise. Then John Bartram announced that a decision had been reached.

A merchant. William, the artist and botanist, would be apprenticed as a merchant. James Child, a former ship captain, had a store near the waterfront in Philadelphia. Here, William would learn how to keep accounts in business. With many new stores opening throughout the colonies, it seemed a wise choice. John had made his decision, but William felt betrayed.

William Bartram knew he had talent in art and botany. He had rave reviews about the drawings sent to his father's friends. The talented sixteen-year-old, however, had also been taught to respect his parents. He started work at the store. Of course, whenever he had a free minute, he was in the nearest corner, drawing sketches on any scrap of paper.

Peter Collinson complimented the young man's talent over and over. Collinson wrote to John: "... I am very sensible of the great pains Billey has taken about the Turtles – I can't reward him Equall to his Merrit I send him a Small Token & some fine Drawing paper...the Marsh Hawk is admirable I don't see that either Edwards or Ehret can much excell it ...."[6] What a compliment! George Edwards and George Ehret were well-known wildlife artists in England.

Peter Collinson soon felt guilty encouraging William at his drawing. To make up for his guilt, he sent William a book that might help him in his career, *A New Introduction to Trade and Business.*

Hoping that his son would get over his misery and make the best of his opportunities, John Bartram went on with his own work. He and his son Johnny made a trip south to Virginia and the Carolinas, where they were welcomed into Dr. Alexander Garden's Charleston home. Fascinated by the wide variety of plants, the two explorers would leave each day at dawn, returning each evening with many interesting wild southern plants. After eighteen exciting days of exploring, they traveled to North Carolina to visit with John's half-brother, William, who was living at Ashwood, his plantation near Cape Fear. After a pleasant reunion, John and Johnny borrowed horses and rode home.

Keeping delicate southern plants alive in Pennsylvania was another challenge. In 1760 John built a small greenhouse so that his plants would be safe from the cold winters. He wrote to Collinson in 1761: "... I can chalenge any garden in America for variety ...."[7] That same year, however, John climbed a tree to collect holly berries and a branch cracked beneath him and sent him to the ground. In tremendous pain, John called for help. For weeks he could hardly pull his shirt over his head to dress himself, but that didn't stop him from planning another trip. He hoped to go to Pittsburgh the following fall.

William, in the meantime, was not thriving at all. George Edwards, the English wildlife artist, had used some of William's bird drawings as models in his books, *Gleanings of Natural History,* and *A Natural History of Uncommon Birds*, and had sent William copies. He did not acknowledge the gift.

When his Uncle William suggested that the 21-year-old come to North Carolina to stay at Ashwood, William jumped at the chance.

What a break for William. He was warmly welcomed into his uncle's home, where he described his new life: "... here no Preaching."[8] He opened his own trading store along the Cape Fear River, bringing some goods from Pennsylvania that might sell there. The venture was financed with some of his father's money, and although this type of store was sometimes successful, William's was not. He still did not like working as a merchant, but at least now his father couldn't watch him, couldn't constantly give advice. For several more years William plodded on, making an effort at the store, and doing his drawing whenever possible. Postage for letters was expensive, so he seldom wrote to his parents.

Chapter 5
The King's Botanist

By 1763, there was news about new land to explore, in the North, West, and South. The Treaty of Paris was signed in February of 1763, ending the long French and Indian War, and transferring most of French Canada and French Louisiana east of the Mississippi River to Great Britain. Spanish Florida would also become a British territory. John read the news, and he dreamed.

John Bartram was no longer a young man, but at age 63 he was still very eager to travel. He was recommended for several trips. He considered going with Colonel Henry Bouquet to explore the lands around the upper Mississippi River, but news of Indian uprisings in the area postponed that trip. A painful ulcer on his leg held him back from traveling anywhere else. When a doctor's medication did not heal the ulcer, John tried his own medicine and it was more successful. As soon as he felt better, he thought about a trip again, and the longer, the better.

England was very interested in Florida. It would be easy to send colonists to the new southern territory, and Great Britain would then have settlers in all the American colonies along the Atlantic Ocean. To govern the area more easily, England split the southern territory into two new colonies. East Florida would be governed from St. Augustine, and West Florida governed from Pensacola. King George III of England wanted information about the region.

In 1764 friends came to John Bartram with news that his neighbor, William Young, Jr., had sent some seeds to Queen Charlotte, the wife of the king, and she had responded by bestowing on him the title of Queen's Botanist. William Young would not only get a title, but he would get enough money to spend time finding plants in the colonies!

Could John, at 64 years of age, become the King's Botanist? He talked over the idea with his friend Benjamin Franklin. Franklin suggested he write to Peter Collinson about his idea, because Peter had so many friends in the English government.

John worked fast. He put together a package of his finest plant specimens for the king, and wrote to Peter, suggesting that he be paid by King George III to explore the new lands. He wanted time enough to make a thorough search and also wanted his son, William, to join him on the trip.

Waiting for an answer seemed to take forever. Offers of other trips arrived, but not his answer from Collinson. He was invited to travel in Canada, into the province of Quebec. Henry Bouquet, now a general, wanted to go to Florida, and invited John to join him. John waited – and waited – to hear from his friend in England.

The good news finally came. After some months, in his letter dated April 9, 1765, Collinson wrote: "I have the pleasure to Inform my Good Friend that my Repeated Solicitations have not been in Vain for this Day I received certain Intelligence from our Gracious King that He had appointed thee His Botanist with a salary of Fifty pounds a Year ...."[1]

John Bartram had been chosen the King's Botanist! The news spread fast through Kingsessing and Philadelphia – and to John's friends all over America and Europe. The money he would receive was not as much as he had hoped for, but John would soon be taking the trip of his lifetime. He was asked to explore the area around the St. Johns River in East Florida, a new territory!

Flowering trees all over Pennsylvania were in full bloom that June 7, 1765, when John wrote an important letter to his son. Would his 26-year-old son consider taking another trip with him? In that letter was the key to open a new door in William's life. William would get out of his store and back to botany and drawing! Here, once again, was a chance for William to use his own talent.

Lives all around were changing, not just William's. While a happy father and son prepared for their trip in 1765, Great Britain, in order to help pay its debts for defending the colonies during the French & Indian War, levied taxes on the colonists. A Stamp Tax was required on most legal and commercial papers. Because the colonists had no direct voice in British government, some cried: "No taxation without representation!" Mobs rioted in New York and Boston. Colonial businesses closed rather than comply with the unwanted tax, and some agreed not to import any British goods. Feeling that their rights were being violated, some of the colonies united in New York at the Stamp Act Congress. The reaction to the Stamp Tax surprised Britain's King George III.

William was still in North Carolina, so the King's Botanist joyfully sailed south in early July 1765 with General Henry Bouquet. Arriving in Charleston, John and Bouquet parted. John visited with Dr. Garden and another friend, Henry Laurens. Taking another day to just enjoy the bustling city with its brick marketplace and shady oak trees, John readied himself for the next part of his trip. Nicely rested, John traveled to Cape Fear, North Carolina, to meet William, and the two returned together to prepare for their journey into Florida. They met several people who might help ensure their safety as they traveled. Dr. Garden introduced them to Colonel John Stuart, the superintendent for Indian Affairs in the Southern Department. Stuart promised to do whatever he could to promote a friendly reception in the area they wanted to explore.

The two travelers went farther south into Georgia, having dinner with the governor of the colony, Sir James Wright, and taking the time to explore the Savannah River inland all the way to Augusta. Moving south again along the Georgia coast, on October 1st John wrote in his journal that they saw a very curious shrub he did not recognize in a swampy area near the Altamaha River. When John wrote that something was curious, it was interesting to him. When he wrote that it was *very* curious, the find was fascinating. These shrubs were not in bloom, and it was too late in the year for seeds, so they had to go on their way without satisfying their curiosity.

On reaching the Florida territory, the two travelers crossed over the St. Johns River and followed the Old Post Road, also known as the Savannah to St. Augustine Road, reaching the oldest city on October 11th. There, John was stunned to hear that his friend Henry Bouquet had died of a fever in Florida just a month before.

Because John and William were taking this trip on behalf of the King of England, letters of introduction to important people had been sent in advance of their arrival. Unfortunately, the letter to the new governor of East Florida, James Grant, did not arrive, but Governor Grant was so impressed by the Bartrams that he made them welcome. Grant commissioned two men to go with the travelers on their exploratory trip; one to be hunter and guide, and the other to be cook and in charge of the dugout canoe.

After dinner with the governor, father and son explored Saint Augustine. They had heard a lot about the Spanish town, and both were fascinated with the unusual architecture of the houses and the Castillo de San Marcos, the old Spanish fort. Mosquitoes were ever present, and John became sick with a fever, possibly malaria, while in Saint Augustine. He rested for a while and recovered.

The two travelers headed for Fort Picolata on the St. Johns River for a conference with the Creek Indians, by invitation of Governor James Grant, who also attended. Property lines were an issue again, and a treaty signed on November 18th, 1765, established a new boundary for East Florida. Because John had observed the ways of northern Indians, he was very interested to meet some Native Americans of the South. He also wanted to look for wild plants in the Indian territory, so he and William stayed very busy. Leaving St. Augustine at the end of December, father and son and their guides finally headed towards the St. Johns River.

"Slept but little,"[2] was often written in John's journal. Warmer weather brought terrifying thunderstorms. Indians were a constant threat. Wolves were heard howling on the 10th of January. At their overnight camp on January 15th they killed a 400-pound bear. John found the bear meat to be mild and sweet. By mid-January 1766, they had reached the thick reeds that were at the headwaters of the St. Johns, and could go no farther. They were close to what is now called Titusville, and started back down the river the next day. On January 24th William discovered another new species of a flower they had seen before. They had seen a purple star anise, but here William discovered a star anise that was yellow. The whole tropical world was new and tremendously exciting to both travelers.

John Bartram's Journal
Courtesy: The Historical Society of Pennsylvania

John and William followed the St. Johns River, the only one in Florida that flows from south to north, its whole length, nearly 400 miles, down one side and up the other. When they came to a creek flowing into the river, they often followed the creek to see where it ended. John wrote all the details in his journal. He described how the river meanders, tested depths of the water where possible, and observed the soil all along the way. The date, time, weather, and types of plants they saw were recorded accurately and diligently.

William drew pictures of plants and animals, and Peter Collinson wrote in May 1766 that: "Billys Elegant drawings are admired by all that see them...Mr Ehret our famous flower painter was with Mee & I showed Him Billys paintings, He admired as Wee do all...His Butterflies, Locust are Nature itself his yellow Fly is admirable ...."[3]

When they arrived back in St. Augustine, John had many stories to share with Governor Grant. Grant gave him a room where he could prepare a map of the St. Johns from his sketches along the way, and to add some notes to his detailed journal. For the next month he would be very busy writing, mapping, and preparing plants. John Bartram's *Account of East Florida* was published in London in 1767. While John was working, however, William realized how much he had become enchanted with Florida.

Their whole nine-month trip had been successful. An exhausted John Bartram was eager to return to Pennsylvania. He had been sick several times and he was tired. He was also worried about the news from Philadelphia. The Stamp Act was repealed in 1766, but then the Declaratory Act was passed, stating that the English government had the right to make laws for the American colonies. Thoughts of independence would soon follow this unhappy course of events.

Chapter 6
Endings and Beginnings

In Florida, thoughts of independence were in someone else's mind already. William Bartram announced to his father, as gently as he could, that he could not go back to the North, or back to a store, after their fascinating trip through the Florida wilderness. The young man had made a decision. He would stay in Florida.

John Bartram was tired, so tired, but he clearly heard the determination in his son's voice. William chose to be a planter along the St. Johns River. With no previous experience at farming in the South, William wanted to try his hand at growing rice and indigo, a popular southern crop used as a rich, deep blue dye.

What could John do? He could see no hope for success, but William was now an adult and would not be talked out of his decision. He could only make sure that William had the necessary items for survival. John bought land along the St. Johns River and provided tools and seeds. Because plantations were based on slave labor, John was expected to buy some slaves to help with the work. Money was left with a storekeeper nearby so that William might buy two cows and two horses. Red and white yams, rice, corn, salt, and much more was sent to help William survive until his own crops could be harvested.

On March 17, 1766, John left St. Augustine with a heavy heart, headed for Charleston. He spent twenty more days in that area while visiting with Dr. Garden and packaging specimens and William's drawings for the king. It was hard to tell his Charleston friends about William's decision to stay in Florida. Those who knew William's artistic talent were horrified to hear that he had set aside that budding talent to become a Florida planter.

John finally arrived home on April 22, 1766, after his longest absence yet, with feelings of both happiness and despair. Johnny had done an excellent job of filling orders for Peter Collinson, who congratulated the young man, saying that the fall shipments had all arrived safely and well packed. John told the family about William, and then wrote to Collinson. "I have left my son Billy in florida," John wrote, "nothing will do with him now but he will be A planter upon St. Johns river about 24 mile from Augustine ...."[1]

William was not worried. He was finally happy that he had made a decision for himself, and was relieved to see his father leave. It was not, however, the last he would hear from his father. Still wanting to be helpful, John sent letters telling his son how to catch fish, how to plant lime trees, and other information he could find. He signed his letters, "thy loving father."[2] William did not write back. He was quite a distance from a post office.

John stayed busy packaging the remainder of the more than 250 varieties of plants he would send to the king. Knowing how hard it was for his son to get mail through to him, John just hoped for the best. Again, he had to rely on letters from friends to let him know about William.

From the Collections of the SC Historical Society

Henry Laurens
Courtesy: South Carolina Historical Society

Henry Laurens, a planter who sometimes took business trips in the South, visited East Florida and twice stopped to see his friend's son. On the first visit, Laurens found William sick with a fever. Laurens gave him some advice on planting in the South. On a second visit three weeks later, William was still sick and his crop had been ruined by heavy rains. The young man had tried, but the venture lasted less than a year. It had been too much for him. The slaves had been no help, perhaps because the whole idea of slavery went against William's firm Quaker upbringing.

> **Slavery** – Servants performed part of the work at the Bartram Garden, but they were treated with respect, as part of the larger family. Quakers believe in equality of all people, regardless of race or gender.

John soon was informed of what was happening. Laurens sent John a letter about "...the forlorn state of poor Billy Bartram,"[3] describing the conditions under which William was living. The plantation was on a poor piece of land nine miles away from the nearest neighbor. William was living in a miserable little hut, with hardly any food to eat, and the slaves were more of a problem than a help. William himself had appealed to Laurens to write to his father, telling him of his sorry situation.

Laurens sent some tea, cheese, biscuits, and other foods to William. When an answer came from John, they both suggested to William that he leave the land immediately and return home to Pennsylvania. William had failed again.

It was mid-December before the Bartrams heard from another friend about their son, and it was not good news. William had left his plantation, but he had not left Florida. He had gone to work for William Gerald De Brahm, a surveyor. De Brahm was establishing boundary lines for a large new colony started by Dr. Andrew Turnbull, called New Smyrna. When William left that job, he boarded a ship at St. Augustine, and it was reported that the ship had been wrecked. Nothing more was heard of the young man.

John suffered a great sense of loss and guilt. Until they had more definite word, though, he and Ann refused to give up hope. In early 1767, John had a problem with vertigo, serious attacks of dizziness. Some good news about his son helped cheer him. William was alive and well in St. Augustine. When William did finally return to Philadelphia in the fall of that year, he told his parents that, in his desperation, he had even written to Peter Collinson. He hoped that Peter might know of some job, even in London, for him to do. Unfortunately, he had received no reply. "Poor Billy" again had nowhere to go except home, and in shame. He had failed at the career his father had chosen for him. He had failed at the career he had chosen for himself. What was to become of him?

Sending some specimens to Collinson, John again included William's sketches, and again received only compliments in reply. Peter was absolutely convinced of William's superior artistic talent. He was determined to help the young man make a living with his art. Peter sent William some fine drawing paper and set about in earnest to show William's drawings to as many of his friends as possible.

Good news at last! Peter Collinson announced that Margaret Cavendish Bentinck, the Duchess of Portland, was very impressed with William's drawings. Because her hobby was collecting and studying seashells, she ordered drawings of all American shells. She would pay – to William – 21 guineas in British money for the drawings. Also, Dr. John Fothergill ordered some drawings of land tortoises. At last William would be paid for what he really wanted to do.

William himself received a letter from Peter Collinson which said: "When art is arrived to such perfection to copy close after nature, who can describe the pleasure but them that feel it, to see the moving pencil display a sort of paper creation, which may endure for ages, [to] transfer a name with applause to posterity."[4] Collinson had great faith in the Bartrams, both father and son, and his faith in William would not be wasted. Collinson knew even at that time that William's name would be remembered "to posterity."

The warm friendship that lasted more than thirty years and spanned an ocean came to an end in 1768. Collinson became ill of a kidney ailment, and died on April 11th. He had lived a full life, contributing greatly to the scientific learning of his time. And even though they had never met in person, certainly he had done all he could for both John and William Bartram and their careers. John,

William, and many people around the world would be devastated by Peter's death.

The collaboration between John Bartram and Peter Collinson had a great effect on the variety of botanical species in both countries. Among the hundreds of plants that were sent across the ocean, John sent to England varieties of rhododendron, mountain laurel, and azalea, which were very popular. Peter Collinson sent to America lilacs, lilies, and geraniums, among countless others. His son Michael, and later, Dr. John Fothergill and his nephew James Freeman, would help the flow of plants into London, but no one could really fill the void left by Collinson's passing.

John Bartram would continue to receive accolades from around the world for the work that Peter Collinson had aided so well. In late summer of 1769, John received a letter from the Swedish Royal Society that read:

"The Royal Academy of Sciences of Stockholm wished to show in the only way it can how much it regards the merits of the celebrated man JOHN BARTRAM, Royal Botanist in North America of the British Domain, and for that reason it has received this MR. BARTRAM into its fellowship and among the members of the Academy April 26, 1769. Therefore I salute him as a fellow with these presents in the name of the Royal Academy of Stockholm. In evidence of the matter I affix the Large Seal of the Academy,

PETER WARGENTIN
Permanent Secretary[5]

Peter Collinson had been a member of this society. Carl Linnaeus, who formulated his own plant classification system, had been among those who founded the Swedish Royal Society and had been elected its first president in 1739. It was to his friend Linnaeus that John Bartram wrote a thank you letter telling his appreciation of the honor they had bestowed upon him. Linnaeus certainly knew of John's contributions to botany. He had used John's specimens to name many North American plants.

The American Philosophical Society, which had been somewhat neglected over the years, was re-activated, and John, along with two of his sons, Isaac and Moses, became resident members. William, in North Carolina, was elected a corresponding member. Moses Bartram had worked aboard a ship when he was younger, and became the only family member to meet Peter Collinson while he was in London. At the age of 28, Moses returned to Philadelphia and trained to become a druggist at his half-brother Isaac's apothecary shop on North Second Street in the city. While his brothers and sisters were busy with their lives, however, William still had only touched on his real talent and could not seem to settle into a steady career.

Apothecary Shop - Treatment for sickness in colonial days was with herbs or medications meant to bring harmony back to the body. In the Bartrams' apothecary, customers would pay cash or barter with goods. In 1787, two people paid for their treatments with pairs of shoes. One paid with a pair of silver knee buckles.

William worked as a farm laborer and again as a merchant to pay off some debts. After each long day, with tired, aching muscles, he still spent hours, whenever he could, with his paper and pencil. In September 1770, however, William was threatened by one of his creditors and, without a word to his family, disappeared. His family finally heard that he retreated once more to his uncle's house in North Carolina.

When the Bartrams realized the cause of the sudden departure, they paid off all of William's debts. John wrote to tell his son and added: "... thy mother brothers & sisters Joyns with [me] in love to thee & I remain thy affectionate father ...."[6] For William, this was just another embarrassment because he was now 31 years of age and his family still had to help him out.

John couldn't do much more for his son. He couldn't entice him with another trip. At over 70 years of age, the botanist had such bad eyesight that he had trouble seeing the plants in his garden. Benjamin Franklin, who invented bifocal lenses, helped his friend by sending thirteen pairs of new eyeglasses. John was to choose the best ones for his sight now, keep the stronger ones for the future, and give away the rest. At least the glasses helped part of his problem.

John had turned over the farm and nursery business to Johnny, and finally retired from his plant-collecting expeditions at age 71. He still would not be idle. He put some finishing touches on his large stone house, and enjoyed reading by the Franklin stove in a room decorated with pictures of his very good friends: Peter Collinson, Benjamin Franklin, George Edwards, and Carl Linnaeus.

Still the King's Botanist, John continued to send specimens to King George III. In with other plants he sent two frogs – live frogs. He sent them to Dr. Fothergill who was to forward them to the king, and was told that the "... frogs came safe and lively"[7] to England. Unfortunately, the king had other matters on his mind, like problems with his unruly colonies, to fuss with frogs at the time.

The botanist also reserved a part of his garden so that he could still do some experimenting. Benjamin Franklin, in England where he was representing the colonies, sent some seeds of rhubarb, turnip, soybeans (with a recipe for tofu), and cabbage turnip (kohlrabi) seeds for John to try. Would the seeds grow in Pennsylvania? John would find out.

Still in North Carolina, William was also experimenting. At the age of 33, he was thinking deeply about his life and was ready to make a stand.

Chapter 7
Peace – and a Revolution

In the middle of a hot summer in 1772, a letter arrived from William, this time *telling* his parents what he wanted to do with the rest of his life. He would absolutely not work as a merchant. That was not an option. Instead, he said, leaving no room for doubt, he was determined "...to retreat within myself to the only business I was born for, and which I am only good for..."[1] William was determined to free the talent within him.

Unfortunately, William also mentioned in the same letter that he resolved to go to Florida again. This time, John could hardly restrain himself. He was happy with the determination in William's letter, but to go back to Florida? The idea was ridiculous. John would put no money into this venture; no, not again. In the reply to his son, John told William to come home, where his family and friends would help him find work.

William would not go back to his family. Not now. William wrote a letter to Dr. John Fothergill in London, enclosing some of his drawings. He asked outright if Dr. Fothergill, who had bought his drawings before, would now finance a trip to Florida.

Dr. Fothergill had to think about this proposal. He was very busy with his medical practice, but knew he could have a more interesting garden himself if he had some new plants from America. Collinson again came to mind. He had inspired Fothergill's love of plants. Collinson had given him some of his own fascinating seeds, and the fun and excitement of collecting was contagious. Fothergill also felt an obligation to help the Bartrams now that their mutual friend was gone. And — William Bartram's drawings had been so highly recommended.

Would William consider going to Canada instead? Fothergill knew that it would be more practical if he had some plants that would not be harmed by cold English winters. William stayed with his own plan. He would go to Florida.

Still intrigued by the tropical world of Florida and having faith in William's talent, Dr. Fothergill told the young man in 1772 that he would finance a trip through the South. In a letter to William's father, Fothergill explained his decision: "A few weeks ago I received a letter and some drawings from thy Son William in Carolina For his sake as well as thine, I should be glad to assist him. He draws neatly, has a strong relish for natural History and it is pity that such a genius should sink under distress...He proposes to go to Florida It is a country abounding with great variety of plants and many of them unknown."[2]

William's life was about to take a new turn.

Dr. Fothergill suggested that William take a trip for as long as two to three years. He should collect seeds, live plant specimens, and make drawings of everything interesting, but all drawings must be done from life. Fothergill would pay William the same amount as his father had received as King's Botanist, fifty pounds sterling a year in British money, plus shipping expenses and extra for each drawing. Dr. Lionel Chalmers of Charleston would be William's contact in the South. William Bartram would now be paid to draw and collect plants, but he would also be on his own, experiencing life on his own terms.

There was a tearful and happy reunion when William returned briefly to Pennsylvania before the start of his new enterprise. John and Ann were thrilled with their son's happiness, and also wondered where this new venture would take him. Sadly, but hoping for the best this time, they again said good-bye as he left on March 20, 1773 on his trip south.

William would later write about his feelings as he boarded the ship headed for Charleston: "How supremely blessed were our hours at this time! ...under no control, but what reason and ordinate passions dictated, far removed from the seats of strife."³

There may have been peace in William's life, but the peace in America was about to explode. Rumblings of revolution were here and there, but they grew louder, bloodier, and firmly united. In March of 1770 there had been a confrontation between colonists and British troops, later called the Boston Massacre. Other taxes were repealed, but the colonists were still required to pay a tax on tea. On December 16, 1773, the colonists rebelled by dumping boxes and boxes of British tea into Boston harbor. Britain closed the port of Boston and placed Massachusetts under the control of a military governor, Thomas Gage.

Benjamin Franklin and John Fothergill and many others on both sides of the Atlantic thought it might still be possible to live peaceably as English colonies. Would war be necessary? One thing was clear: the colonies needed to work together. Patrick Henry said: "The distinctions between Virginians, Pennsylvanians, New Yorkers, New Englanders are no more. I am not a Virginian but an American."⁴ The next few years would be critical for all.

The ship taking William to Charleston was racked by storms, but the young artist made the most of his time. In the wind and rain, a small bird evidently lost its way and fell to the deck of the ship. William drew the little finch, and upon his arrival in Charleston on March 31, 1773, gave the drawing to Dr. Chalmers, his contact in the South. Duly impressed, Chalmers wrote to John shortly after William arrived in South Carolina: "...indeed it surprises me, that you should not have encouraged this Genius of his as a Naturalist sooner..."[5] Chalmers predicted, even at that time, that William would keep the Bartram name alive in the history of scientific discovery.

William rested before taking a smaller boat to Savannah, Georgia. There, William was again welcomed by the governor, Sir James Wright, and was invited to another meeting with Indians, this time in Augusta, Georgia. William chose to make the side trip because of his fascination with all of the Native Americans, and also because he wanted to be introduced to the Indian chiefs to assure his safe passage through the South. He later said: "... it proved of great service to me."[6] On May 1st, William and a friend, John McIntosh, the son of Lachlan McIntosh of Darien, Georgia, traveled to Augusta in the company of Indians and government officials.

The two travelers were amazed at the large number of Indians at the meeting. William had not seen such a huge group together since the meeting at Fort Picolata with his father. There were about 300 Creek, and 100 Cherokee. At this meeting, the Native Americans agreed to the Treaty of 1773, drawing new boundary lines between the territories for not only the settlers, but also the Creek and Cherokee tribes. Because some of the Indians were unhappy with the terms of the treaty, John Stuart warned William about going into Indian territory at that time.

William and McIntosh explored the area around Augusta, finding several new plants. Near the rapids along the Savannah River he found a shoals spider lily, and near the Broad River he found the Piedmont rhododendron.

Here William also saw "... the most magnificent forest I had ever seen."[7] The gigantic oaks made him stare in disbelief. The forest had been undisturbed for many years, and "... many of the black oaks measured eight, nine, ten, and eleven feet diameter five feet above the ground ...."[8] He commented that no one would believe his tale of seeing trees this size.

William's mind was open to everything: sights, feelings, fragrances. On a hillside on the way back from Augusta his foot slipped and he started to fall, grabbing onto whatever shrubs he could reach along the way. He wrote later, not of his own safety, but about the smell of one of the plants that had come out by its roots and "... filled the air with animating scents of cloves and spicy perfumes."[9]

Returning again to McIntosh's home in Darien, Indian problems and illness delayed his trip farther south. Lachlan McIntosh had already made the traveler very welcome when he arrived, saying: "Friend Bartram, come under my roof, and I desire you to make my house your home, as long as convenient to yourself ...."[10] The family helped him back to health, and by November he was sufficiently recovered to pack some specimens, take them to Savannah, and send them off to Dr. Fothergill.

The traveler made the rest of his trip alone or in the company of various guides along the way. Traveling alone allowed him to totally relax and enjoy his freedom and his surroundings. He found once again the curious shrub that his father had seen several years earlier and took the time to draw it for Dr. Fothergill. He absorbed the beauty of every day.

Later, in his book *Travels*, he described a sunset after canoeing during the day on the Altamaha River: "The glorious sovereign of day, clothed in light refulgent, rolling on his gilded chariot, hastened to revisit the western realms."[11] And while camping beside the Altamaha one night, there was a lunar eclipse and William was right there to witness the marvelous sight. He would later write about the spectacular sight: "lo! A dark eclipse of her glorious brightness came slowly on."[12] William was permitting himself to feel all the artistic emotion in his being.

Chapter 8
"Puc Puggy"

Finally arriving in Florida, William bought a boat for sailing on the St. Johns River. The scenery was somewhat familiar this time, but he still enjoyed the magnolia trees with their dark green leaves and buds ready to bloom, and the majestic cypress trees with moss hanging from their branches. He described the crystal springs as having water so clear that "... you may without the least difficulty touch any one of the fish, or put your finger upon the crocodile's eye, when it really is twenty or thirty feet under water."[1] (It was really an alligator he meant – these creatures were new to William.)

While gathering plants in some woods, William was "... greatly surprised at the sudden appearance of a remarkably large spider on a leaf...at sight of me he boldly faced about, and raised himself up, as if ready to spring upon me ...."[2] Getting over the shock of having so large a spider so close, William, quite naturally, was curious as to what the spider was doing. It seems he was after a fat bumblebee, and the spider would "... leap nearer, and then instantly retire out of sight, under a leaf or behind a branch, at the same time keeping a sharp eye upon me."[3] The spider got his meal when the bee was more interested in sipping the nectar from a flower than watching out for his enemies. William watched the whole event, totally fascinated.

By mid-April 1774, William traveled along the St. Johns River, stopping where he had also stopped with his father, at Spalding's Lower Store near Palatka. Because trading boats traveled regularly between his Upper and Lower Stores, James Spalding, the owner of the busy stores, kindly provided transportation for William when needed. Continuing on his journey and traveling inland for a while with some traders headed towards the Indian village of Cuscowilla (near present-day Gainesville), William saw another absolutely amazing sight.

After traveling through thick, dark woods, William suddenly saw the huge flat plain of the Alachua Savanna spread out before them, and was amazed at its beauty. He described the scene for us later: "Neither nature nor art could any where present a more striking contrast, as you approached this savanna. The glittering water pond played on the sight, through the dark grove, like a brilliant diamond ... bordered with various flowery shrubs and plants ...."[4]

At the village of Cuscowilla, Seminole Chief Cowkeeper treated the men to a banquet of soup, stew, and barbecued ribs. Cowkeeper listened carefully as William explained his mission. William was there only to collect and study plants, and was as respectful of the land as the Indians themselves. Chief Cowkeeper could see the peaceful nature of the young man, and gave William "... unlimited permission to travel over the country for the purpose of collecting flowers, medicinal plants ...."[5] The Seminoles would further honor him by giving him an Indian name: "Puc Puggy," or Flower Hunter.

During May and June of 1774, William continued his travels in Florida. He explored Blue Springs, the Suwannee River, Manatee Springs, and the area around Lake George, and had another close call. Camped on the shore of the lake, he heard a noise at midnight. Jumping up, he saw a wolf running off with the remains of his supper. He had hung some leftover fish from a branch of a high bush, and then gone to sleep under that same bush. The wolf had come within a couple feet of William's sleeping head!

William continued his journey through Florida, on and around the St. Johns River, following paths here and there, collecting plants and noticing every detail wherever he went. By November he was ready to leave, and again shipped some specimens to England.

The first two years of his trip were over, and William had reached a turning point in his life. He no longer thought of himself as a failure. In March 1775, William finally sent off a letter to his father. "Honord & Benevolent Father," the letter began, "I am happy by the blessing of the Almighty God by whose care I have been protected & led safe through a Pilgrimage these three & twenty months till my return to Charlestown two days since." and was signed, "... ever your faithful son."[6] The two years had finally matured the restless young man. However, he was still not ready to come home. William stated very clearly: "... I am resolved with the concurence of Doctr Chalmers to continue my travels another year."[7]

William had explored East Florida. He was ready to move on, ready to see more of the South. William traveled hurriedly through Savannah and Charleston, where the populace was anxiously reading the news about events taking place in the Massachusetts colony. History was unfolding rapidly as British General Thomas Gage and his men embarked on a march from Boston Common towards Lexington and Concord. In April of 1775, Paul Revere and others were hastily riding to warn of the approaching English troops.

That same April, William was in a more peaceful world. Having decided to see the Great Smoky and Appalachian Mountains, the traveler was content to be in the deep woods again. William expected to have a guide on this trip, but when his guide didn't arrive, he made the trip into Cherokee country anyway. He was taking his chances, because he was a colonist going into Indian land. He enjoyed the awesome beauty of the scenery there, later describing what he saw as he reached the top of a hill: "... a vast expanse of green meadows and strawberry fields; a meandering river gliding through...fruitful strawberry beds; flocks of turkies strolling about them; herds of deer prancing...or bounding over the hills."[8]

William always had to be on guard, however, reminding himself that this was Cherokee Indian territory. The quiet of the deep woods was split one day by the sound of a group of Indians, on horseback, coming directly towards him. His sharp eyes recognized the Indian at the head of the group. It was Ata-cul-culla, Little Carpenter, brave chief of the Cherokees.

Showing respect to the approaching Indian party, William turned his horse off the road to allow the group to pass. The chief returned the courtesy to William, clasping his hand to his chest and then offering his hand to William in friendship. He said: "I am Ata-cul-culla."[9] He asked William if he had heard of him, and William replied yes, adding that he was from a tribe of white men who respect the Cherokees. Here again, William's peaceful and respectful ways would allow him to pass through safely, but he only spent one month in Cherokee territory.

William was fascinated with all Indians. Once it was obvious that he was not after their land, he traveled in safety through the Cherokee and Creek Nations, and actually lived among the Seminole. He wrote down notes on their customs, games, and lifestyle. The adventurous son had not accepted his father's fear of Indians. In school, William was influenced greatly by a teacher, Charles Thomson, who believed that the Native Americans should be respected, not chased out of their native land. William believed that everyone and everything on earth had its own reason for being, and its own purpose in the whole scheme of life.

William respected animals, as well. The woods were filled with many varied creatures – wildcats, cougar, wolves, gray and red foxes, porcupines, rats, gophers, and plenty of snakes. There were so many of each species that often William couldn't sleep because of all the forest noises. The loud grunting of alligators in a swamp, the thousands of birds settling down for the night on branches nearby, or the loud buzzing of the thousands of mosquitoes, made it very hard to relax at times. As annoying or dangerous as these animals could be, William still hated to see any killed, except a few for food.

Having made the decision to see the Mississippi River, William turned his eyes west. His father had wanted to see the great river, but hadn't made it that far west. The Mississippi was the great dividing line at that time: to the east was colonial America; to the west was almost totally unexplored wilderness. By June 22, 1775, William joined a company of traders bound for the city of Mobile, in West Florida. His Mississippi trip covered about 1,200 miles in eight months, and almost cost William his life.

After many stops along the way and seeing fascinating new scenery and plants, William and his party arrived in Mobile. There, William fell ill with a dreadful fever, possibly from a poison ivy infection or scarlet fever. His own knowledge of medicinal plants saw him through the illness this time, and he began to recover. Governor Peter Chester of West Florida had heard that John Bartram's son was in the area, and requested his company in Pensacola. Feeling better, William sailed across the clear waters of Mobile Bay to Pensacola for a short visit in early September.

William was still determined to see the mighty Mississippi River. Boarding a trading ship from Mobile, he again headed west. But the mysterious fever returned, even worse than before. William's eyes became extremely sensitive to daylight and hurt so intensely that he could not sleep. The ship stopped at a plantation on the Pearl River, and the critically ill young man was taken to the home of a settler along the river who had medicines. William had no choice but to rest from mid-September through mid-October. It took weeks before he could open his eyes without pain, and his left eye never did regain its former strength.

Finally able to travel again, however, William did not give up. He would see the Mississippi River. Traveling by ship and overland, he made it to the Baton Rouge area, where he met a fellow lover of nature, William Dunbar. Throughout his trip, this peaceable traveler usually met people who were extremely hospitable, and at just the right times. Here he was in luck again. Dunbar, a very learned person, a friend of Thomas Jefferson's, and a member of the American Philosophical Society, was acquainted with William's father. Dunbar became William's traveling companion along the Mississippi River. The sight of the mighty Mississippi River was truly a healing sight for sore eyes. William Bartram would remember this experience for the rest of his life.

It was finally time to head home. In November of 1775, William left Baton Rouge and his new friend, again sending off drawings and specimens to Dr. Fothergill. William headed northeast, realizing that his body was not as strong as it had been before his strange illness. Arriving back in Savannah in late January 1776, William visited some of the friends he had made, thinking he might not see them again. Stopping at Darien, it was no longer the peaceful place he remembered. The woods here were no longer safe.

Riding his horse quietly at sunset near the St. Mary's River, William saw an Indian crossing the path ahead. Because the Seminole had a rifle in hand and looked very angry, William ducked behind some trees. No use; he had been spotted. The Indian turned his horse and raced straight towards the terrified, defenseless young man. There was no chance to run. The traveler had never been so afraid of an Indian. With no alternative, William became quiet, resigning himself to whatever might happen.

Regaining his peaceful composure, he stood very still, looking the Indian in the eye. This "intrepid

Siminole,"[10] startled by this lack of fear, was in for another shock. William stepped towards him and offered his hand in greeting, calling him brother. At first the Indian pulled back, but then, realizing that this was one white man who would harm no one, the Indian confidently thrust out his hand in peace. William asked the way to a nearby trading post. The Indian answered. Both men went on their way.

Very curious as to the cause of the Indian's anger, William learned at the trading post that the Indian had been mistreated. The Seminole had ridden off fiercely angry, with rifle in hand, saying that he "… would kill the first white man he met."[11] Another close call for the traveler!

There were even more dangers in the previously peaceful woods. The Declaration of Independence had just been signed in Philadelphia, and British soldiers were in Georgia, near the McIntosh plantation. William probably did some scouting for the American soldiers in that area, reporting on where he had seen British outposts. Arriving back at Darien, the McIntosh family, along with William, prepared to leave the coast for the safety of Savannah. William Bartram was headed home.

John and William Bartram: Travelers in Early America

Chapter 9
Safe and Sound

An illness almost took his life. An Indian almost did the same. A wolf came within a foot of his head. William's journey had not been dull. His trip had lasted almost four years, covering approximately 2,400 miles. He had traveled by foot, horseback, canoe and a primitive sailboat. He had hunted, fished, and gratefully accepted meals with settlers and Indians along his way. He had sent more than 200 dried plants and 59 drawings to London. His travels towards his career, and into manhood, would soon be over.

William stopped in Charleston and sent a package to Dr. Fothergill, in which he included the report of his trip. He visited Dr. Chalmers, who was very happy to see William safe and sound. Dr. Fothergill had written several times asking about William, but no one had heard from the traveler. British soldiers were expected back in the Charleston area, alarming the townspeople, so William left quickly for a short visit to Cape Fear, then headed for home.

By Christmas he reached Virginia, and the icy cold weather made William shiver as he made the best time he could through deep snow. Approaching the Susquehanna River, he found it ice-clogged and had to look for a safe place to cross. He may have stopped to see his twin sister Elizabeth and her family in Lancaster County on his way home, and in early January 1777, William finally approached the door of his father's warm home in Kingsessing.

William returned home a new man, and he returned home to a new country. While William Bartram had been busy defining his life on his own terms, the Americans were also defining themselves as a nation.

News of the fighting at Lexington and Concord in 1775 had been somewhat expected, but it took some colonists by surprise. The colonists were still divided. Some remained loyal and devoted to the British king, while some realized that independence could be an answer to the problem of British rule. Opinions were also divided in England. Some felt the colonists had a valid grievance. Dr. John Fothergill wrote to John Bartram in 1774: "Do not imagine that all the people in this country are against America. We sympathize with you much."[1]

To decide their united course of action, the First Continental Congress convened in Philadelphia in September of 1774, and the Second Continental Congress in May of 1775. Henry Laurens of South Carolina was elected president of the Continental Congress. George Washington of Virginia was chosen on June 15, 1775 to be the commander-in-chief of the American army.

Thomas Jefferson of Virginia was asked to draw up a draft of a document stating their determination to be free and independent. By the 4th of July, 1776, the Declaration of Independence was adopted. There was no turning back.

William Bartram had come home from his trek through America's wilderness to a whole new world. Battles would rage for several more years, but the tension in William's life was gone. The area near Kingsessing was battleground during the American Revolutionary War, and John Bartram greatly feared for his garden. General Howe and his British troops occupied Philadelphia, but the garden – and the Bartrams – were spared.

John Bartram was 77 years old and in frail health when his son William returned home that cold January day. Immediately John and Ann noticed the change in their son. He was thinner, and not in good health, but his head was held high. William was no longer a failure, but a successful man. John was happy now to sit and listen to his son's many adventures.

One of William's first stories, especially for his father, was about the mysterious shrub that John did not recognize on their trip together to Florida. On his way home, William remembered to return to that place by the Altamaha River in Georgia, and saw a magnificent sight. He found several of the shrubs, full of spectacular white blossoms, but also bearing ripe seeds, some of which William was able to gather for his father. Later, in 1784, William would name the curious shrub the *Franklinia Alatamaha*, (the old spelling of the river Altamaha) for their friend Benjamin Franklin, and for the place in which it was found. The Bartrams helped save the *Franklinia* from extinction. It was seldom found in the wild after that time.

Franklinia Alatamaha - The Franklinia was an outstanding discovery of the Bartrams. The tree has not been found in the wild since 1803 and every Franklinia seen today probably derived from those that William grew at the Bartram Garden. The Franklinia is an example of the damage done when natural vegetation is destroyed.

Franklinia Alatamaha
Courtesy: The Natural History Museum, London

One story after another came out of the relaxed young man. He told of the changes around the St. Johns River. A large Indian mound they had seen together was now gone, leveled to make room for farms and roads. Farmers had cleared out many of the beautiful old orange groves. Hunters had cleared the forests of some of its wildlife. William had watched as a large bear was killed by a hunter, and felt the pain of a smaller bear, unafraid of the gun, as it "...approached the dead body, smelled, and pawed it, and appearing in agony, fell to weeping and looking upwards, then towards us, and cried out like a child."[2]

There were still plenty of alligators, however, and William explained how he almost became their supper one evening. Camping on the shore of Lake George in Florida, William decided to catch some trout for his supper, and "... two very large ones attacked me closely...roaring terribly and belching floods of water over me. They struck their jaws together so close to my ears, as almost to stun me, and I expected every moment to be dragged out of the boat and instantly devoured."[3]

William barely escaped. For the rest of his life William had nightmares about the alligators in "Battle Lagoon,"[4] and John breathed a sigh of relief that his son had returned safely.

William Bartram's drawing of alligators
Courtesy: The Natural History Museum, London

John Bartram soon realized that his son's trip had not been just a wild idea, but extremely worthwhile. William had returned with much new information about the plants, geography, and even the Indians, of the South. John and William Bartram were now two men who had both accomplished what they wanted to in life, and they became close friends again in the precious months they had together in 1777.

John Bartram was alert and active until a short time before he died on September 22, 1777. He was buried in the Darby Friends Burial Ground, but news of his passing was slow to reach his friends because of the British soldiers occupying the city of Philadelphia during 1777-1778. Only after the danger was past were friends able to write or stop by the Bartram home to fully express their sympathy. Carl Linnaeus had earlier called John Bartram the "...greatest natural botanist in the world,"[5] and truly this man, who added so much to gardens and scientific knowledge around the world, would be missed.

Business was slow in the garden during the war, but a package of seeds and plants from the Bartram Garden was given to Sieur Gerard, the French Ambassador. France had sent troops to help the colonists, so the Ambassador was pleased to return to his country with some unusual American plants.

When the British troops surrendered on October 19, 1781, peace and optimism finally returned to America. The final treaty of peace was signed at Paris, France, on September 3, 1783, ending the

American War for Independence. The new country's western boundary was the Mississippi River.

Ann Bartram had lived to see peace again in America. She died in 1789, but the Bartram heritage would go on. With the war over, William helped his brother, Johnny, to re-start the nursery business. William worked on bookkeeping and putting together lists of available plants. The first printed plant catalog in America was issued in 1783 for Bartram's Botanical Garden, and the 1784 catalog even listed the *Franklinia Alatamaha*. The *Franklinia*, which had grown without trouble in Bartram's garden, was one of over 200 varieties of shrubs and trees for sale at that time.

The catalogs continued to grow. By 1807 the catalog was 33 pages long, included 1,500 plants, and even had a history of the garden written by William. Orders came from all over. Plants were sold to Mount Vernon, George Washington's home; Monticello, Thomas Jefferson's home; and Independence Hall in Philadelphia. One of the *Franklinias* was even sent to the Palace at Versailles in France.

Dr. Fothergill died on December 26, 1780. His passing, too, was mourned by his many friends in America, as well as in England. Benjamin Franklin, who knew Dr. Fothergill and had been treated by him when he became ill on a visit to England, said of this caring scientist: "I can hardly conceive that a better man existed."[6]

William gave some thought to returning to Florida to do more research on his book or taking a trip with his brothers to the Mississippi River, but those dreams were shattered. In his late 40's, William was climbing a tree to gather seeds when he fell and fractured his ankle. Just lucky to be alive after the severe pain of the compound fracture, William used a cane for the rest of his life. With both eye and leg problems now, his traveling days were over.

Chapter 10
Travels

Deciding to use his father's first-floor study as an office, William cleared aside some of the varied collections of pottery, pinned butterflies and moths, and many notebooks, so that he would have a place to write down what he had experienced on his southern travels.

It would never be a dull room, though, just as the quiet woods had never been dull. A pet opossum would wander by occasionally. William's old dog usually slept quietly at his feet, but Tom, his pet crow, was a constant nuisance. Tom tried constantly to get William's attention, but if William did not look up from his work, Tom would steal anything he could off the desk. Eyeglasses, pen, whatever – would go flying out into the garden. There, Tom flew from tree to tree waiting for a limping William to follow him.

William's writing now would not be in the scientific language of a report or journal such as he sent to Dr. Fothergill. This would be totally *his* book and he was free to write as he pleased. The title would be a long one because it contained so much information about what he had experienced: *Travels through North and South Carolina, Georgia, East and West Florida, the Cherokee Country, the Extensive Territories of the Muscogulges or Creek Confederacy, and the country of the Chactaws. Containing an Account of the Soil and Natural Productions of Those Regions; Together with Observations on the Manners of the Indians.*

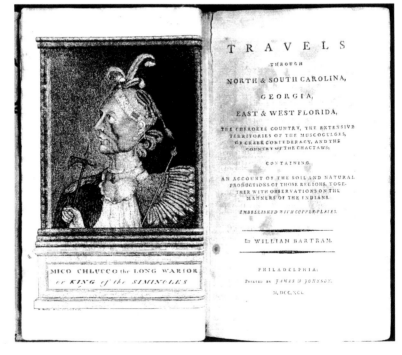

Travels, by William Bartram
Courtesy: The John Bartram Association, Historic Bartram's Garden

William savored each beloved memory. He had plenty of time now to find exactly the right words to describe the wonders he had seen. He carefully went over all the notes on little scraps of paper saved from the trip. Some scribbled thoughts were on old drawing paper. Some were on backs of envelopes. On his way north William had left a trunk filled with his papers and specimens in Charleston with a friend. When that arrived at the Bartram home after the war, William had even more information with which to write. He had lots of information, especially in his very imaginative mind.

He didn't have to follow anyone else's rules, so William's individual style of writing broke new ground. He wrote as an artist would write, painting a picture so that the reader might *see* the scene as he describes it. No one gave advice to this man anymore. This was an honestly emotional man writing about the beauty of nature.

William divided his *Travels* into three parts, with a fourth part about the fascinating Indians. *Travels* is the story of a life-changing journey, through woods that were as fascinating as they were dangerous. The truth about the Creeks, Cherokees and Seminoles is also told, clearly and bravely describing them as a people native to this land who deserve respect and understanding.

Some dates are wrong. Some facts might be wrong. The book was called a work of art by some people, a work of science by others. Readers were delighted to find both in *Travels*. Some thought the stories must be exaggerated. Others simply allowed themselves to become entranced by the very obvious emotion and sense of wonder that flowed from William's words. Facts intermingle with awe, weaving together science and feeling. *Travels* can amaze the reader even in our day, when it is considered a classic work of literature.

A formal description of soil or the geography of the area is suddenly interrupted with: "O thou Creator supreme, almighty! how infinite and incom-prehensible thy works! most perfect, and every way astonishing!"[1] William's Quaker belief that nature is God's handiwork fills the book with a spirituality not usually seen in nature writing.

Nature is alive. William, the artist, wrote so that his readers might share in his wonder. He paints the picture of a sunset with the words: "Behold...the pendant golden Orange dancing on the surface of the pellucid waters, the balmy air vibrating with the melody of the merry birds, tenants of the encircling aromatic grove."[2]

There is no plodding through this wilderness. The reader experiences the peace of an evening near the St. Mary's River: "It was drawing on towards the close of day, the skies serene and calm, the air temperately cool, ...fragrant shrubs, filled the air with the richest perfume. The gaily attired plants which enameled the green had begun to imbibe the pearly dew of evening; nature seemed silent ...."[3]

When the English poets William Wordsworth and Samuel Taylor Coleridge read *Travels*, they realized that this was not just a travelogue. This was poetry. Another author might have written that birds were singing, but William wrote that "... their songs seem to be musical compositions ...."[4] William was doing more than sharing facts. He was admitting us into his world. He was uncovering soaring, majestic feelings evoked as he traveled within a magnificent, magical place that, unfortunately, was soon to disappear.

We feel William's awe; we feel his discomfort. While trying to sleep one night: "Our repose however was incomplete, from the stings of musquetoes, the roaring of crocodiles, and the continual noise and restlessness of the sea fowl, thousands of them having their roosting places very near us, particularly loons of various species, herons, pelicans, Spanish curlews, etc. all promiscuously lodging together, and in such incredible numbers, that the trees were entirely covered."[5]

And the absolute terror of a thunderstorm can bring fear to our own hearts: "How purple and fiery appeared the tumultuous clouds, swiftly ascending or darting from the horizon upwards! they seemed to oppose and dash against each other; the skies appeared streaked with blood or purple flame overhead, the flaming lightning streaming and darting about in every direction around, seemed to fill the world with fire...What a dreadful rushing and roaring there was every where around me!"[6]

William Bartram wrote as an artist, from his heart. The purpose of his journey had surely been fulfilled. As he clearly states in his *Travels,* I am "... continually impelled by a restless spirit of curiosity, in pursuit of new productions of nature, my chief happiness consisted in tracing and admiring the infinite power, majesty, and perfection of the great Almighty Creator ...."[7] William had not run away into the wilderness; this man had to experience life fully so that he would be able to share his own perception of the fantastic beauty of nature with others.

His was the voice of a new generation. John Bartram had been a seeker at a time of reason and enlightenment, finding and labeling nature; William took a more romantic approach, looking to find beauty and spirituality in the nature around him.

A journal was kept through the years, following his father's example. Each day he carefully recorded date, weather, and assorted facts. He wrote down the date that the first daffodils pushed through the snow in the spring, when the apples were ripe in the fall, and that he was totally surprised to hear a catbird singing in his garden in the middle of winter.

William became an authority on North American birds. He compiled a list of 215 native birds, and stated whether or not they were permanent residents of Pennsylvania. He was also the first to keep a calendar of bird migrations, and even possibly put bands on the legs of birds to note their migration patterns.

Some people tried to tempt William out of his peaceful garden. In 1782 he was offered the position of Lecturer in Botany at the University of Pennsylvania. William did not do any lecturing. President Thomas Jefferson asked William to accompany some explorers on a pioneering trip into the western territories. At over 60 years of age, William said he was too old.

He was not too old, however, to notice what was happening in Philadelphia, which would be the nation's capital for ten years. During the hot summer of 1787, delegates at a Constitutional Convention debated ways of governing the new states. The Constitution of the United States was adopted on September 17th when a new, very unique, government had been chosen for the brand new United States of America. The American wilderness was changing even as William was writing his book. George Washington was inaugurated as the first President of the United States of America at a ceremony on April 30, 1789 in New York. Many people from all over the world would soon come to find new opportunities in the new, independent America, and the wilderness would quickly become just a part of our history.

Travels was published in 1791, by publishers James & Johnson of Philadelphia. Secretary of State Thomas Jefferson was one of the first to buy a copy. The next year, *Travels* was printed in London, England, followed by editions in other European languages. Some European editions, however, were printed without William's knowledge and so he did not make any money from those sales.

Chapter 11
A Fruitful Garden

William Bartram chose not to leave home, but many came to the Garden. George Washington visited on June 10, 1787. Several weeks later a large group of members of the Constitutional Convention, including James Madison and Alexander Hamilton, made an unannounced visit to the Bartram Garden. Thomas Jefferson visited as often as he could, along with many others. Even the Bartrams' old southern friends, Lachlan McIntosh and Henry Laurens, came to visit.

William did not dress up for his guests. They often found "The Traveler" (as they called him then) out in the garden, barefoot and dusty, but he would always take time for a chat with his friends. William Dunlap, a playwright, wrote of his experience during a visit to William in his garden:

"Arrived at the Botanist's Garden, we approached an old man who, with a rake in his hand, was breaking the clods of earth in a tulip bed. His hat was old and flapped over his face, his coarse shirt was seen near his neck, as he wore no cravat or kerchief; his waistcoat and breeches were both of leather, and his shoes were tied with leather strings. We approached and accosted him. He ceased his work, and entered into conversation with the ease and politeness of nature's noblemen. This was the botanist, traveller, and philosopher we had come to see."[1]

William gave freely of his time to others seeking information and advice. Benjamin Smith Barton, who became the Professor of Botany at the University of Pennsylvania, spent a lot of time at the Bartram garden before he wrote the *Elements of Botany*. William contributed many of the illustrations for this work, which, when it was published in 1803, became the first botany textbook in America. The *Elements of Botany* was such an important book that it was taken on Lewis and Clark's journey to the northwest in 1804.

Alexander Wilson, who once called William's garden a paradise, often asked for help in identifying the birds of Pennsylvania for his *American Ornithology*. William not only gave him help with the birds, but also with his art. In November 1803, Wilson wrote to William: "Dear Sir, I have murdered your Rose. I traced the outlines with great patience but in colouring and shading I got perfectly bewildered."[2] William Bartram spent many hours with Wilson so that he would "murder" roses no more. Wilson was tremendously grateful to William for his help.

Thomas Nuttall, who collected plants in the Rocky Mountains, spent so many hours in the botanic garden that they called one room of the house "Nuttall's Room"! Andre Michaux, called the "French Wanderer," visited William several times, and his son Francois spent time with William as well.

William Bartram, portrait by Charles Willson Peale
Courtesy: Independence National Historical Park

His father had received honors for his work, and William received his share, as well. He was a member of the American Philosophical Society and was elected to other learned societies in both Europe and America. He was elected to the newly formed Academy of Natural Sciences of Philadelphia, and Charles Willson Peale, popular artist of the day, came to the Garden to paint William's portrait. Peale was collecting portraits of famous men for his new museum.

Truly, John and William Bartram had lived at a remarkable time, but their lives also were remarkable. They worked through fears, illnesses, and career decisions, but neither of these two men ever gave up.

William spent his last days in peace, at home and in his garden. He owned very little – just his clothes, his feather bed, and a few other items. He had never married. He went to bed about 10 o'clock each night, and rose each day before daybreak. He once wrote: "To know ourselves is to know what sort of creatures we are, what is our duty and business and what we shall be."[3] William was finally happy. He knew he had fulfilled the dream of his own life.

On a warm, clear summer day, having just finished writing the description of a plant, William decided to go for a walk in the garden. A blood vessel burst in his lungs, and he died, with relatives right nearby. It was Tuesday, July 22, 1823, and William Bartram was 84 years of age.

Earlier, Alexander Wilson said the words that sum up the life of the man who was finally able to share his joy in life and nature. He had written that, because of William Bartram: " ... I see new beauties in every bird, plant, or flower, I contemplate."[4] And John Livingston Lowes wrote "William Bartram exemplified that rarest of combinations: the mind of a scientist with the soul of a poet."[5]

John and William Bartram were father and son, but they were very different people. Both changed, grew, and prospered in their own chosen professions. Both saw the American colonial settlements change and grow and be transformed into the United States of America. Both traveled through much of early America. Both encountered many setbacks. But both firmly kept their eyes on their goals, and their lives became a part of world history.

The philosophical writer and naturalist Henry David Thoreau, whose book *Walden; or, Life in the Woods*, was published just thirty-one years after William Bartram's death, wrote words that would describe the Bartrams' lives so well. He said: " ... if one advances confidently in the direction of his dreams, and endeavors to live the life which he has imagined, he will meet with a success unexpected in common hours. He will put some things behind, will pass an invisible boundary .... "[6]

John and William Bartram, father and son, will not be forgotten.

John and William Bartram: Travelers in Early America

Afterword

John Bartram thought his son would not be able to make a living at art, but by the end of William's life, many Americans had careers as artists. Right in Philadelphia, Thomas Sully was a portrait painter, William Rush was known for his wood sculpting, and Charles Willson Peale, just two years younger than William Bartram, was an internationally known portrait painter. Peale, while painting William's portrait in 1808, was also busy setting up exhibits in his new Pennsylvania Academy of the Fine Arts.

Roads, widened and paved, brought many new settlers to fast-growing Philadelphia. In 1804 a permanent wooden bridge spanned the Schuylkill River. No longer would adventurers going west have to depend on a ferry or floating bridge here. Recent research shows this bridge had a plaque on it heralding agriculture, and it may have included the likenesses of William Bartram, as well as Carl Linnaeus, sculpted by William Rush.

Medicine changed dramatically. John Bartram and the doctors of his day relied on plants for healing. By the end of the seventeenth century there was an excellent medical school at the University of Pennsylvania. The Pennsylvania Hospital, started by Benjamin Franklin and the Junto, was recognized for excellence in medical research.

Even plant collecting changed rapidly. In John Bartram's day, plants from the "New World" of

America were new and fascinating. By 1800 Captain James Cook's ships had sailed around the world and then plants were desired from the latest "new worlds." Protection of the environment came next, with naturalists John Muir, founder of the Sierra Club; Marjory Stoneman Douglas and the Friends of the Everglades; and President Theodore Roosevelt preserving land for national parks.

John and William Bartram had been in the right place at the right time, and became a part of America's history. One can still step back into their world, however, by visiting the Historic Bartram's Garden in Philadelphia, Pennsylvania.

Entrance to Historic Bartram's Garden
Courtesy: Sandra Wallus Sammons

Ann Bartram Carr, William's niece, and her husband, Colonel Robert Carr, lived at the Bartram home in William's later years, taking care of him. A well-educated woman, Ann Carr was trained as an artist by her Uncle William. The Carrs cared for the garden until it left family hands in 1850. The garden and its National Historic Landmark house is now a Philadelphia park property operated by the John Bartram Association in cooperation with the Fairmount Park Commission, open to the public and to scholars from around the world. Our fascinating past can be just a plane ride away.

Sandra Wallus Sammons

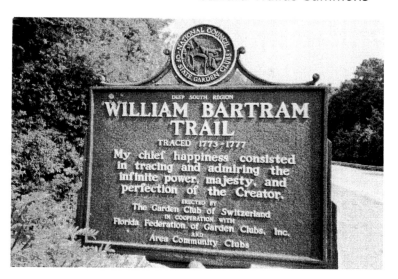

Bartram Trail sign in Florida
Courtesy: Frank Gromling

If You Want to Know More

If you would like to visit:

Historic Bartram's Garden
54th and Lindbergh Blvd.
Philadelphia, PA 19143
215-729-5281

At the Garden, some of the original buildings from John Bartram's day are still standing. Guides in 18th century dress will point out the elegant architectural style he chose for his house. The columns on this house may be the oldest columns in the United States. There's a restored cider press down by the river. What was once a 300-acre farm is now about only 46 of the original acres, but it is painstakingly being brought back to what it may have looked like when the Bartram family lived there. A bird refuge is also a part of Historic Bartram's Garden.

On becoming a member of Historic Bartram's Garden, one can also receive the very informative *Bartram Broadside* periodically, published by the John Bartram Association.

If you'd like to visit via the Internet:

Go to: www.bartramsgarden.org

Local organizations:

The Bartram Trail Conference, Inc. was created in the mid-1970s and there are groups in many states. Their web site is www.bartramtrail.org Along with their attempts to identify and mark Bartram's southern trip, they also promote the creation of recreational trails and botanical gardens along the route. Many people have walked where the Bartrams walked (or close to it), following guidebooks and "Bartram Trail" signs.

For further reading about John and William Bartram, and their period in history:

Bartram, William. Travels, NY: Literary Classics, 1996.

Berkeley, Edmund and Dorothy Berkeley. The Correspondence of John Bartram, 1734-1777. Gainesville: University of Florida Press, 1992.

Cashin, Edward J. William Bartram and the American Revolution on the Southern Frontier. Columbia: University of South Carolina Press, 2000.

Leckie, Robert. George Washington's War: the Saga of the American Revolution. New York: Harper-Collins, 1992.

Sanders, Brad. Guide to William Bartram's Travels. Athens: Fevertree Press, 2002.

Footnotes

Chapter 1 – Beginnings in a New Land

[1]Pennsylvania State Archives web site, www.docheritage.state.pa.us/documents/charter.asp

[2]M.S. Tyler-Whittle, The Plant Hunters, (New York: Lyons & Burford, 1997), p. 57.

Chapter 2 – Growing Gardens and Friendships

[1]Letter, Collinson to John Bartram, February 17, 1737/38, The Correspondence of John Bartram, 1734-1777, ed. Edmund Berkeley and Dorothy Smith Berkeley, (Gainesville: University Press of Florida, 1992), p. 84.

[2]Letter, Collinson to John Bartram, April 10, 1767, ibid., p. 684.

[3]Letter, Collinson to John Bartram, October 10, 1759, ibid., p. 473.

[4]Letter, Collinson to John Bartram, February 3, 1741/42, ibid., pp.180-181.

[5]Letter, Collinson to John Bartram, December 20, 1736, ibid., p.36.

[6]Letter, Collinson to John Bartram, June 11, 1762, ibid., p 562.

[7]Letter, Collinson to John Bartram, March 20, 1736, ibid., p 26.

[8]Letter, Collinson to John Bartram, March 3, 1741/42, ibid. p. 186.

[9]Letter, Collinson to John Bartram, April 27, 1755, ibid., p 381.

[10]Robert Elman, First in the Field: America's Pioneering Naturalists, (NY: Mason/Charter, 1977), p. 29.

Chapter 3 — "All in a Flame"

[1]Letter, John Bartram to Colonel Byrd, probably summer of 1739, Berkeley and Berkeley, p. 120.

[2]Letter, John Bartram to William Bartram, probably early summer of 1761, ibid., p. 518.

[3]Letter, John Bartram to Collinson, October 23, 1763, ibid., p. 612.

[4]Letter, John Bartram to Collinson, July 22, 1741, ibid., p. 163.

[5]Letter, John Bartram to Templeman, July 6, 1761, ibid., p. 525.

[6]Letter, John Bartram to Collinson, late winter or early spring 1745, ibid., p. 251.

[7]Edmund Berkeley and Dorothy Smith Berkeley, The Life and Travels of John Bartram: From Lake Ontario to the River St. John, (Tallahassee: Florida State University Press, 1990), p 139.

[8]Ibid, p. 129.

Chapter 4 — William, "my little botanist"

[1]Letter, Collinson to John Bartram, July 19, 1753, Berkeley and Berkeley, p. 350.

[2]Letter, John Bartram to Collinson, August 20, 1753, ibid, p. 354.

[3]Letter, John Bartram to Collinson, fall of 1753, ibid, p. 360.

[4]Letter, John Bartram to Collinson, September 28, 1755, ibid, p. 387.

[5]Letter, John Bartram to Collinson, April 27, 1755, ibid, p. 384.

[6]Letter, Collinson to John Bartram, February 18, 1756, ibid, p. 398.

[7]Letter, John Bartram to Collinson, July 19, 1761, ibid, p. 529.

[8]Letter, William Bartram to John Bartram, May 20, 1761, ibid, p. 516.

Chapter 5 – The King's Botanist

[1]Letter, Collinson to John Bartram, April 9, 1765, Berkeley and Berkeley, p. 644.

[2]Thomas P. Slaughter, The Natures of John and William Bartram, (NY: Vintage Books, 1996), p. 105.

[3]Letter, Collinson to John Bartram, May 28, 1766, Berkeley and Berkeley, p. 667.

Chapter 6 – Endings and Beginnings

[1]Letter, John Bartram to Collinson, June 1766, Berkeley and Berkeley, p. 668.

[2]Letter, John Bartram to William Bartram, July 3, 1766, ibid. p. 670.

[3]Letter, Henry Laurens to John Bartram, August 9, 1766, ibid, p. 672.

[4]Edward J. Cashin, William Bartram and the American Revolution on the Southern Frontier, (Columbia: University of South Carolina Press, 2000), p. 3.

[5]Berkeley and Berkeley, p. 281.

[6]Letter, John Bartram to William Bartram, July 21, 1771, Berkeley and Berkeley, p. 745.

[7]Letter, Fothergill to John Bartram, January 13, 1770, ibid, p. 750.

Chapter 7 – Peace–and a Revolution

[1]Berkeley and Berkeley, p. 285.
[2]Letter, Fothergill to John Bartram, undated, but written in September or October 1772, Berkeley and Berkeley, p. 750.
[3]William Bartram, Travels, pp. 108-9.
[4]Patrick Henry, from a speech given at the First Continental Congress, Philadelphia, October 14, 1774, inscribed on a plaque in front of Carpenters' Hall, Philadelphia.
[5]Letter, Chalmers to John Bartram, April 7, 1773, Berkeley and Berkeley, p. 759.
[6]Bartram, p. 33.
[7]Ibid, p. 55.
[8]Ibid, p. 55.
[9]Cashin, p. 64.
[10]Bartram, p. 37.
[11]Ibid, p. 64.
[12]Ibid, p. 65.

Chapter 8 – "Puc Puggy"

[1]Bartram , p. 151.
[2]Ibid, p. 22.
[3]Ibid, p. 22.
[4]Ibid, pp. 100, 101.
[5]Ibid, p. 165.
[6]Letter, William Bartram to John Bartram, March 27, 1775, Berkeley and Berkeley, pp. 768, 770.
[7]Letter, William Bartram to John Bartram, March 27, 1775, ibid, p. 770.

[8]Bartram, p. 291.
[9]Ibid, p. 297.
[10]Ibid, p. 43.
[11]Ibid, p. 44.

Chapter 9 – Safe and Sound

[1]Letter, John Fothergill to John Bartram, July 8, 1774, Berkeley and Berkeley, p. 765.
[2]Bartram, p. 20.
[3]Ibid, p. 115.
[4]Ibid, p. 119.
[5]Ellman, p. 26.
[6]Cashin, p. 246.

Chapter 10 – *Travels*

[1]Bartram, p. 71.
[2]Ibid, p. 50.
[3]Ibid, p. 43.
[4]Ibid, p. 23.
[5]Ibid, p. 79.
[6]Ibid, p. 131.
[7]Ibid, p. 81.

Chapter 11 – A Fruitful Garden

[1]Slaughter, p. 246.
[2]Letter, Alexander Wilson to William Bartram, November 10, 1803, Life and Letters of Alexander Wilson, ed. Clark Hunter, (Philadelphia: American Philosophical Society, 1983), p. 204.
[3]Slaughter, p. 251.
[4]Ibid, p. 252.

⁵Dorothy Sanger, <u>Billy Bartram and His Green World</u>, (New York: Farrar Straus & Giroux, 1972), p. 189.

⁶Henry David Thoreau, <u>Walden</u>, (Boston: Beacon Press, 1997), p. 303.

Index

About the Author

Sandra Wallus Sammons is a former elementary school librarian who saw a need and filled it. When teachers asked for biographies about key people in American history, she discovered that few existed for the young reader.

Her biographies about Henry Flagler, Marjorie Kinnan Rawlings, Jacqueline Cochran, and Marjory Stoneman Douglas have transformed Sandy from a librarian into an award-winning writer of historical biographies.

John and William Bartram: Travelers in Early America is her first book for the 8th grade reading level, and it is by far her most ambitious and successful work to date. She remains dedicated to helping teachers enliven the study of history in our schools through factual and inspiring biographies.

The author resides with her husband and two cats in Edgewater, Florida and is now at work on her next biography.

John and William Bartram: Travelers in Early America

Ocean Publishing
Quick Order Form

Fax orders: 386-517-2564. Send this completed form.
Telephone orders: Call 888-690-2455 toll free in USA.
Have your credit card ready.
E-mail orders: orders@ocean-publishing.com
Postal orders: Ocean Publishing, Orders Department, P.O. Box 1080, Flagler Beach, Florida 32136-1080, USA.
Telephone 386-517-1600.

Please send me the following order of _John and William Bartram: Travelers in Early America_:

Quantity	Price/Book	$Total	
_____	**$14.95 Softcover**	$ _____	(USA)
_____	**$19.95 Hardcover**	$ _____	(USA)
	Sales Tax*	$ _____	
	Shipping**	$ _____	
	Order Total	$ _____	

*Sales Tax: Add 7% for orders to Florida addresses
**Shipping: Add $3.45 for first book and $1.85 for each additional book.

Payment Method: Check (# of enclosed check_____)
Credit Card ___Visa ___Mastercard ___Discover
Card Number: _____ Exp. Date: _____
Name on card: _____

Name: _____
Street/P.O. Box: _____
City: _____ State: _____ Zip: _____
Telephone: (___) - _____ E-mail: _____

Please send free information about:

☐ Other books   ☐ Author speaking
☐ Author Events